# My Life
## in a
# Nutshell

Donna Shogren

ISBN 978-1-64468-391-0 (Paperback)
ISBN 978-1-64468-392-7 (Digital)

Covenant Books, Inc.
11661 Hwy 707
Murrells Inlet, SC 29576
www.covenantbooks.com

My name is Donna Lou. I was born at 1:00 a.m. on December 22, 1938, in the little village of Cornell, Wisconsin. I am the youngest child and the only girl in a family of three. I had two older brothers: Richard Lee, born on November 19, 1930; and Neil Duane, born on February 5, 1937. Our parents were Carl Joseph and Mabel Lillian Rose Magnussen; we were a normal family for a few years until tragedy struck when I was four years, eight months, and four days old. My mother died from leukemia on August 18, 1943. She was thirty-four years old.

The next few years were very difficult for me; the welfare was going to put Neil and me in an orphanage. Reluctantly, our maternal grandmother decided to take us. When we were taken from Dad and brought to Grandma and Grandpa's place, it was so difficult. Everyone and everything was strange to us. When we misbehaved and someone tried to correct us, Grandma would say, "Leave them alone. They are poor little orphans." It didn't take long for us to become incorrigible little brats. Grandma never believed in spanking, but she used some terrible words against me, like I killed my mother and that if I misbehaved, I would kill her too. Words that cut deep. Soon I got a thick skin, and I wouldn't let anyone get close to me, so the words won't hurt; I am still that way today.

Before we left Cornell and moved to Minnesota, we spent some time with Mom's three brothers and their families. Uncle Frank and Aunt Violet had two daughters in my age bracket. Shirley was a little older, and Dottie was a little younger, so I fit in there okay. I stayed there until I was moved to the next family.

I wrote a poem about Uncle Frank. It goes like this: "Whenever I think about Uncle Frank and I often do, I get a happy feeling to the bottom of my shoes. He treated me like a daughter even though I was his niece. He paid us girls to comb his hair, and we got a penny piece."

Uncle Frank was Mom's oldest brother. When he came home from work, he would let us comb his wavy hair. Shirley first then me and then Dottie. He died on June 14, 1954. He was fifty-three years old. They lived on a farm east of Cornell. They had horses and cows and other animals. Uncle Frank worked at the paper mill in Cornell. He died driving his car; he never crashed it. He had a massive heart attack, but he managed to stop his car before he died. He and Aunt Violet had a blended family—his, hers, and theirs. They included Art, Reuben, Audrey, Glen, Donald, Shirley, and Dottie.

Uncle George was Mom's second brother. He was okay as long as he was sober. When he drank, he got real nasty and cruel in his words. I remember he used to take us kids to the Rock Inn Tavern. Back then, soda pop was five cents a bottle. I would ask him for a nickel for a bottle of pop, and he would grumble about supporting other people's kids; he said he had enough of his own. I think my skin got thicker because of the way he talked to me. He and Aunt Eunice had seven children. They were George Jr., Harold, Robert, Ruby, Betty, Norma, and Helen.

Uncle Ralph was the third brother; he was our singer and guitar player. He used to make up paradise of other people's songs; I think I got that ability from him. He sounded like Hank Williams Sr.; he sang a lot of Hank's songs. My mother played the guitar and sang songs. I often wonder if she had lived, she would have taught me.

Uncle Ralph and Aunt Marian had three children: Bill, Ronald, and Delores. All three Rose brothers, Aunt Edith's husband, Clarence Webster, my dad, and maybe Grandpa Rose worked at the paper mill. Uncle Clarence and Aunt Edith had one daughter named Dorothy. Aunt Edith left Clarence and lived with Lawrence Stevens; they had three boys—Roger, George, and Gary. Roger was born July 2, 1936. George was born December 18, 1939; and Gary was born November 4, 1945. George and Gary are both deceased. Those three boys were as close and/or closer than my own brothers, especially my older brother Dick. I didn't see him very often. We were like the four amigos: Roger, George, Neil, and I. We were born in 1936, 1937, 1938, and 1939. All four in forty months; only Roger and I are left.

Grandpa and Grandma Rose were married July 20, 1900, in Harwood, North Dakota. Grandma was born December 7, 1879. I don't know Grandpa's birth date, but he was eighteen years older than his wife. So grandma told me he died in 1930. They had five children who grew to adults. One boy was still born. The children were born in this order: Frank, Edith, George, Mabel, Edward, and Ralph.

This is the order of the birth and death of my parents and brothers:

Mabel Magnussen: December 30, 1908–August 18, 1943
Carl Magnussen: February 20, 1903–December 30, 1970
Richard Magnussen: November 19, 1930–May 21, 1971
Neil Magnussen: February 5, 1937–December 30, 2003

Neil was thirty-three years old when Dad died; when Neil died, he was sixty-six years old. This is the founding members of my family on my mother's side; I'll get into Dad's family later on and also the Harvey side of the family. Grandma was a Harvey girl. She had four sisters and one brother. As far as I know, Grandpa Rose had one brother, William, and one sister, Charlotte, nicknamed Lottie.

Grandma and Grandpa Magnussen has a family of five children: Carl, Arthur, Martha, and Alice and Elsie (twins). More details on them later.

My brother Dick and his wife, Alice, had no children. My brother Neil has one with his first wife and five with Paula, his second wife. I had two children with my only husband, Ruben. My daughter Dianne and my son Daniel, the genealogy of the Harvey-Rose-Magnussen families are something else.

I can account for seven generations of the family. Danny has been e-mailing a member of the Rose family. He can trace more generations back, so that is ten generations.

I'll leave the rest of this page blank until Chuck has a family and the girls, Angil and Melina, do in the future.

## Grandpa Stevens

Grandpa Stevens was a quiet, gentle man. I never saw him angry. He pretty much ignored me, except I recall I had a bicycle and I dropped it anywhere I got off it. He warned me the next time I did that, I'd lose the bike. I did, so I lost it. That was a hard bike to pedal, so I didn't mind because my cousin had a new monarch bike. George bought the bike with money he earned picking string beans for a factory. I wonder what happened to that bike.

I remember when my cousin Gary was born on November 4, 1945; he was born with a cleft lip, so he had to have his lip repaired when he was very young. We had to suck on the nipples on his bottles to soften the nipples so he could suck and get his formula. I was about six years old, and George was about five years old. We thought that was fun, at least for a while. Gary was a cute little guy; he died at the age of fifty-five.

Grandma didn't live long after Uncle Frank died; it was such a shock to her. I think she just gave up. When she died, her blood sugar was so high they couldn't test it. Uncle Frank died June 14, 1954, and Grandma died September 21, 1954. In 1945, Grandpa inherited $1,800 from an uncle of his that died. Grandpa took his money and bought a Ford tractor and the attachments that came with it, a plow and a cultivator, I think. I used to walk out to the field and tell him supper was ready. I used to steer the tractor back home. I wrote a poem about it:

Grandpa's Tractor

When I was a child in 1945,
Grandpa got a tractor.
He taught me how to drive.
I'd go and get him out in the field.
And to drive that little tractor,
To me was quite a deal.

Every time I see a tractor like that, it brings happy memories. We lost Grandpa during a horrible blizzard two days before Thanksgiving in 1952; I had to hold him on the chair where he died from a massive heart attack. The doctor told Grandma he couldn't have saved Grandpa's life even if he had been in our house. The telephone lines were down; we had to wait for the milk man to come to get us some help. I wasn't quite fourteen years old. That was the first death of someone close to me since my mother's death nine years earlier.

I always regret not helping Grandpa more. I could have fed the calves or help feed the cows and chickens, but Grandma always told me not to trust any men. She had me so cared of my own father. I wouldn't ride in the car 4 miles from home. I had to have someone else along before I would go. Neil went back to Cornell and Dad when he was about fourteen years old. I was told he called Grandma the b—word, but he told me in 2000 or so that he beat up on Ray Stevens because Ray was beating up on his cousin George, who was quite a bit younger and smaller. Neil came to George's rescue. Neil's leaving never bothered him; he never got along with Grandma anyway; he was glad to leave. Neil went into the army when he was sixteen. Dad signed for him to go; he was in the army for over twenty years.

Uncle Lawrence and Aunt Edith and their boys moved to the other farm in 1948. Grandma and Aunt Edith never got along. Grandma was so mean to her, and she took her anger and frustration out on Aunt Edith and, to a certain extent, on me. She got leukemia and she died, so it was my fault. Back in 1943, leukemia wasn't a well-known disease. About the only thing they could do was blood transfusions and hypos for the pain. I don't know how long she was sick. Grandma never told me. But the things she told me affected me badly for many years, especially my sense of self-worth. Grandma was the kind of person that when you die, you became a saint. You could be the meanest, foulest person that ever lived—but that all disappear when you died. So it was quite a shock to me when I found out Mom wasn't an angel. I was brainwashed into believing she was. I can still hear in my mind Aunt Edith telling Grandma, "You had better tell her the truth, or someday she will find out. And it will destroy her." I found out the truth, and it darned near destroyed me. The only memories I have of my mother are very rare. I remember seeing her walking across the lawn to get me when I was playing in the dirt in the street. There were very few cars in those days. I remember Dad taking me to St. Joseph's hospital in Chippewa Falls to see Mom.

Donna        Katie, stepmother   Dad                    Neil
                    Taken Sept 1953.

I got scared when Dad sat me on the bed that was raised up high. I can see her sitting on a couch reading a book. I can see her in her casket in her blue dress with white polka dots. I reached for her, and Dad jerked me back. That affected me and the way I felt about death until my father's death in December 1970. I told my step-mother I wanted to touch him, but I was afraid to. She picked up my hand and placed it on Dad's hand that took away my fear.

During deer season in 1970, my dad and my oldest brother came to our farm. A few weeks later, I talked to Dad, and he thanked me for the good time he had and said he was coming back the next year for deer hunting. But on December 30, 1970, he died of a massive heart attack. On May 21, 1971, my oldest brother Dick died. He was forty years old; Dad was sixty-seven years old. I drove from my home to Cornell, a distance of about 135 miles. It was 20 degrees below zero, and it was so cold. I went to the funeral home with my stepmother. Something in my mind told me to put a flower in my dad's hands. After fighting that voice for a long time, I asked the mortician if I could put a carnation in Dad's hands. He said I could if I wanted to. Grandma said Dad never supported us kids. After Dad died, I got a wooden chest that had a lot of his papers in it; it also had a bunch of cancelled checks, checks he sent to Grandma for our support. That almost destroyed me too. A few years later, I woke up from a sound sleep with these words in my head. It was close to Father's Day, "You gave your dad a flower." Here is a poem I wrote about it:

You Gave Your Dad a Flower

I gave my dad a flower,
a carnation pure and white.
I placed it in his work-worn hands;
he holds it day and night.

When I think of Dad and that flower,
it eases my troubled mind.
I wasn't always at my best;
at times, I was unkind.

I wasn't raised by my father,
we were many miles apart.
but I hope he knew I loved him;
and he had a place in my heart.

I know someday I'll see him and we'll,
both get a brand-new start.
I'll give him a fresh new flower;
he'll hold that close to his heart.

I was so happy I listened to the voice that told me what to do. In my mind, I see Dad holding that flower, and it will be forty years since I put that flower in his hands. Thank You, heavenly Father. When He guides me, I listen. Amen.

We were never allowed to visit friends' homes overnight or have friends stay overnight. Ann was my good friend, and her brother Floyd was a friend of my brother Neil. I wanted to go with Neil and visit Ann while he visited with Floyd. Neil didn't want me to go. Well, he went and so did I. When it got dark, the boys scared me with horror stories. Neil had a flashlight, but I didn't; and I was too scared to walk home in the dark. At dawn, Grandpa came and got me. Needless to say, we got a sermon on how ungrateful we were and the trouble we caused them.

I don't ever remember my grandma visiting the neighbors or neighbors visiting us although they tried. The neighbor ladies that had berries, raspberries, and strawberries would bring some to our house. Grandma would head for her bedroom and tell me to say she was sick in bed and couldn't visit, so they would leave the berries and go back to their own homes. Then she would leave the bedroom. I hope God forgives me for lying to those ladies; Grandma gave me no choice.

all 8 Classes, District 13 School East Rock Creek Minnesota

Donna Shogren
213 W Burnett Ave Apt. 225
Grantsburg, WI 54840

## Country School

I went to a one-room school; it had all eight grades. I loved that old school. We had a program for every holiday that came along. They were so fun to put on music, skits, and plays; we covered it all. We used to have basket socials. The baskets were bid on by the men in the audience. I was never good at making a basket, but Bud Stevens always bid on my basket; pathetic that it was. God bless that lovely man. He was a treasure; his family was lucky to have him.

We had outdoor outhouses; in the winter, they were not a whole lot of fun to trudge out to. But they served the purpose they were intended for. I wrote a poem about the outhouses.

# Outhouses

In our old country school
That I went to long ago
We had no modem bathroom
We trudged out through the snow

It was not a lot of fun when
Through a snowstorm, we did walk
To answer nature's call
We didn't stop to talk

It was better in the springtime
Snow drifts were no more
We contended with muddy paths
When nature called once more

Those little buildings had their
Place in every child's life
Without them, it would be tragic and
Add greatly to their strife

We would make a skating rink every winter; we had an outdoor pump. The jack handle was awfully cold. We needed good mittens. We had cold lunches, but we had hot cocoa. All of the families took turns with the fixings, milk, sugar, and cocoa. It worked out just fine. Every Wednesday, we had sewing class, embroidery, cross stitch, etc. I enjoyed that and I still do.

It pains me to tell what I have to say next. I was the worst bully that ever lived. I think I was so scared of my grandma and what she threatened to do to me if I misbehaved. That's the only way I could work out my own frustrations—to bully someone bigger and smaller than me and hope they would destroy me because that was what I deserved. The thing that she scared me with was if I had to go to an orphanage or a reform school, she said they had a man who dressed up as a gorilla and he could be under your bed or in the closet in the bathroom, and when you least expect it, he'd jump out and grab you. She terrified me with that threat; I had lots of nightmares from that.

When Grandma was feeling okay and I didn't bother her, we had some good times. She would let me help her wash the old dishes in the curved glass China cabinet. I just loved that, then something would set her off again, and we were back to the abuse again. I learned pretty soon to just stay out of her way. How we survived childhood, I'll never know. We had large beams in the bam. We would swing from the beams with ropes. We rode horses. My favorite was Princess; she was a branded army horse. I think I pulled on the reins because she backed up so much. I wrote a sweet little poem about Princess; she was dapple gray.

Princess

We had a horse named Princess.
She had a sweet and gentle soul,
But she only wanted to go backward,
Which was not my final goal.

The boys Neil and George rode Prince. When he got bit between his teeth, there was no stopping him. He would go under a low branch, duck his head, and brush the boys off of his back and onto the ground; I don't think they ever got hurt though. I was so scared of that horse. When I went to get the cows for milking, he would chase me. I used to throw sticks and rocks and anything else that I could find at him. Grandpa warned me, but I wouldn't listen. One day I was in the pasture. He was across the pasture from me.

14

I thought I was safe. He saw me. I ran for the fence. He chased me around some trees. I got away by the skin of my teeth. After that, I had a lot of respect for Prince and all animals. I don't remember what happened to the horses after Grandpa got his tractor.

We had a dandy sliding and skiing hill across the drive way by our house. It had a nice incline, a nice flat area; but unfortunately, it had a creek at the end of the flat area. In the spring when the snow melted, it was full of water. I never made it to the creek, but I think the boys did. I always sat down before I got to the end. It was fun going down on skis.

## Family Members

When I go back to my *file cabinet*, another name from my mind, I think of some of the characters we had in our family. If we didn't grow them, we married them. One such character was my great uncle, Fred Eastman. He always reminded me of Andy Griffith, not a young Andy, more like a Matlock Andy. He married my great-aunt Julia, Grandma's next older sister. He was about six feet three inches or so. He had a head full of pure white hair. His hair turned white when he was sixteen years old, caused by a real high fever. He would tease Aunt Julia or Aunt Jule, as we called her. He could hold his arm straight out, and she could stand under his arm. He told her when he died, they didn't make coffins that long, so they would have to cut his legs off and lay them beside him. She didn't appreciate that one bit.

I wanted to learn how to ride a bike, so Uncle Fred said he would show me how. So he held on to the bike; he promised he wouldn't let go. I was riding the bike and I looked back, and he was standing and watching me. I was doing okay, but he didn't tell me how to stop. I figured that out on my own. I ran into the silo. I stopped. This was at the other farm Uncle Lawrence and Aunt Edith moved to in 1948.

He used to sell McNess and Watkins products. He had quite a route. They lived in a house close to the Snake River Dam, not far from the Pine Camp Dance Hall. When we would go visit them and we were ready to leave, he would tell us to come back again. He would say, "You know where we live. We live in the dam house." They had one adopted daughter; her name was Ethel Peterson.

He had a fun place to visit. He had a lot of interesting things he made. He would take a 55-gallon barrel, make holes in it, fill it with dirt, and plant strawberries in the holes. That whole barrel was covered with strawberry vines and later, beautiful sweet berries. Yummy. The berries wouldn't rot because they didn't lay on the ground. He had holes in the bottom of the barrel, so he had good drainage. He took the top of the barrel off, so he watered the berries with a garden hose. It worked good.

When he was younger, he was a well driller. He tried to join the *Mason lodge*, but he couldn't get in. He was ineligible for some reason. So he joined the *Odd Fellows*. They took him. He said, "The female half of the lodge was the *Rebecca's.*"

When Uncle Fred and Aunt Jule left Pine City, they moved to White Bear Lake. They wanted to be closer to Carl and Ethel Peterson and the grandkids. Their names were Delores, Joyce, and Robert. They both died in 1962 in January and August. They are buried in the Union Cemetery. I miss them very much.

Great Aunt Hannah Rowan was married to a character also. His name was George Rowan. They lived in Clam Falls, Wisconsin. He would carve puzzles out of a block of wood. I tried for hours to figure out how to take them apart. He would remove one piece, and they came apart. He would put them back together again. He never showed me how he did it, a real puzzle to this day. I love puzzles but not the wooden kind.

Great Aunt Jessie lived in Black Duck, Minnesota. She had a son named Charlie Halstad. He was a politician. I don't know if he was a congressman or a senator. I don't remember him or Aunt Jessie. I do know two of her younger sons, Richard and Earl Gamble. Earl and his family lived in Forest Lake for a short while before they moved to Dawson, Minnesota. I think that was the name of the town. Ron Gamble was married to a girl from Forest Lake. Her last name was Houle. I doubt very much Richard and Earl are still living. They were Mom's cousins, and she would be 102 her next birthday. Aunt Jessie was the oldest Harvey girl.

Great Aunt Maud's first husband was Bill Rose. He was my Grandpa Rose's brother. Grandpa's name was Royal Rose. So two Rose brothers married two Harvey sisters. Bill and Royal had one sister, Charlotte. I know nothing about Bill Rose. Nobody seem to want to talk about him. I don't know if Aunt Maud had three sons that started a country band, the Rose Family Band. Don, Emmett, and David started the band. Don's son Larry is the leader now. Don and Emmett are both dead now. Larry, his wife, Bev, her brother Gary and David—if he is still with the band—are a very talented group.

I am not a very good singer, but I can write lyrics and put music to words. I have four songs recorded. As far as I know, I am the only one in my family who has done that. I have had some of my poetry published. I enjoy writing poetry.

Great Uncle Luther Harvey was the youngest child and the only boy in a family of five older sisters. Grandma was the third girl. She defended her brother from all that had the audacity to say anything negative about him. He married a lady named Sarah Stevens. Uncle Luther was the nephew of Jane Harvey, and Aunt Sarah was the niece of George Stevens. George and Jane were husband and wife. Uncle Luther and Aunt Sarah had four daughters and one son.

Helen was married to John Houdek. They lived off Highway 70, east of Pine City. Ray married Lucille Weber; they lived in Luck, Wisconsin area. Evelyn married Lenny Hill. They lived in Dresser, Wisconsin area. Viola married George Caroon. They lived in Northern Minnesota. Louise lived in Michigan with her husband for many years.

I knew a few of the older kids in the families. I knew Jack and Doreen Houdek, Dorothy, Frank and Patrick Harvey, Allen Ron and Lynn Hill, and Darryl and Sharon Caroon. None of Louise's kids or the younger kids of each family.

Uncle Luther died in 1970 and Aunt Sarah in 1978. I enjoyed being around that couple, especially Aunt Sarah. I was with her quite a bit after Uncle Luther died. I remember after she went in the nursing home, I would help her with her food. She wanted to know what kind of vegetable she had, and I'd tell her string beans. I loved her answer. She'd say, "I ate so many string beans. If they were placed end to end, they would go around the world three times."

I think they were married sixty years or more, which was better than his five sisters. Each one of them was married at least twice and Aunt Maud more times than that. The reason for the multiple marriages was because they married older men.

I remember like it was yesterday when Uncle Luther died. It was ironic how it happened. It amazes me how the good Lord plans events in our lives.

Gertrude Hammergren called me. Her grandson had an accident on the dirt bike. She wanted me to take him to the clinic to get the knee injuries taken care of. While he was at the clinic, I went to the hospital to see Uncle Luther. Vonnie Caroon told me maybe I should bring Aunt Sarah to the hospital. I called her, and she said she didn't think she would come in. I told her what Vonnie told me that death was close. She said okay. I took Jeff home and went to pick Aunt Sarah up. When we got to the hospital, we were met by Vonnie. She said, "Uncle Luther had passed away." She just broke down. I was told later the hospital called and was going to tell her that her husband died. We were on the road, so thank God she didn't get that call while she was alone. She lived about 6 miles from Grantsburg. She was losing her sight, and she lived on a busy highway. If she would have started walking, overwhelmed by grief, what could have happened to her?

Vonnie Ormston Caroon was married to John Caroon, brother of George Caroon who was married to Viola Harvey, daughter of Luther and Sarah. So Vonnie knew the Harveys very well.

## More School Memories

I remember the first time I could throw the ball over the roof of our school house. I remember the ball games between our school District 13 and District 15 that school was on the government road, the old stagecoach trail. Our teacher was Mr. Doyle. District 15 teacher was Mr. Haavisto. I recall the picnics on the last day of school. It was a special time. Hjalmer and Beta Nelson were our janitors. They were brother and sister. The lived the next place west of the school. Their brother Slim Nelson lived in Rock Creek. On a cold winter morning, it was so good to come to a nice warm school. Our little library was in the comer by the stove.

It was my job to get up to Bud and Barb Steven's house to get eggs for the week. We quit raising chickens. Our dog Shep didn't like that idea, so he would go to Allen and Doris Johnson's who lived east of us and steal their laying hens. He never injured or killed any hens. Needless to say, Shep lost his life.

Bud sold their eggs to Shoholm's in Grantsburg. A man named Joe Larson picked up eggs every Saturday morning. So I would go early to pick up the eggs for the week. I would be walking out the driveway. Joe would be driving in. He would shake his finger at me, and soon a package of gum would come flying out of the window. Thank you, Joe. His daughter Elizabeth was married to our veterinarian, Dr. Goodwin Branstad. She lives in Grantsburg.

*Family Matters*

I remember my little cousin Helen Rose came to stay for a few weeks during the summer. I really enjoyed her. I had someone to visit with. We drank milk as it came from the cows, no pasteurizing there. She didn't want milk from cows. She wanted the milk that came from bottles. Helen had two older sisters that came to visit occasionally, Ruby and Betty Rose. They went to a dance at Rush City one Saturday night. They went with a couple of local Romeo's. For some reason or another, they got into an argument, and the girls started walking home about 10 miles away. They were wearing high heels. They finally took the heels off, but gravel isn't very easy on bare feet. They finally found a farmer to give them a ride on a tractor. They soaked their feet quite a while that night.

Their brother made my life miserable when I was a kid growing up. He was real sarcastic and making fun of me. I thought someday I would get even with him. He was like his dad. They both got nasty when they were drinking. In 1985 or 1986, I can't remember, we had a family reunion in Cornell. Typically, Bud had been drinking; he staggered over to me and wanted to know if my husband went deer hunting. I told him that now my husband found me, he didn't need to. I knew what Bud meant; he was referring to the four-legged kind. I was talking about girl friends. He left me alone, but he kept looking at me trying to figure out what I was about. After that, every time I saw him, he treated me with respect. Sure felt good. I actually liked him after that.

## Washday

Monday was washday. What a chore that was. We didn't have water in the house, so I had to get it from the pump outside the bam. I had a milk cart that held 4 to 10 gallon milk cans. I would fill all four cans and push them up the driveway to the house. I had three steps up to the cement deck, and then I carried the water by the pail frill and put it in the copper boiler and heat it on the stove. Then I would transfer the water to the washing machine. At that time, we had a family of seven people. We had no dryer, so I had to hang all of the clothes outside. What a job. We had clothesline all over the front yard. In the winter time, we had frozen clothes. We had lines in the house and dry some at a time. If we were lucky, they would be dry by the next washday. Emptying the washer was easier. We had a drain hose. We had a hole in the wall, put the hose in the hole, and drain the water outside; we had to plug up the hole so no critters could get in.

Grandma had a terrible navel rupture, so she couldn't do much lifting. She did a lot of the ironing, including the sheets. She would never have her rupture repaired because she was afraid if she was put to sleep, she would never wake up. When she was young, she had a real high fever from diphtheria or typhoid. I don't know, but she nearly died. She saw something that terrified her. Grandma died on September 21, 1954. She's in Birchwood Cemetery. Grandpa Stevens's first wife died in 1923. She's in Birchwood Cemetery.

Grandpa and Grandma got married in 1932 after Grandpa Rose died in 1930. There are six graves on that lot. Amanda was buried in the first row, the middle grave. When Grandpa died in 1952, he was buried to the left of Amanda. Grandma was furious;

she wanted them to dig up Amanda, put Grandpa in the middle, Amanda to his left, and Grandma to his right. It never happened, so Grandma was buried to Amanda's right. Grandpa's parents, George I and Jane Stevens, are in the second row. Gary Stevens, grandson and great-grandson, was buried in the third grave. Also Gary's baby brother who was stillborn was buried in George Stevens I grave.

An interesting tidbit about Gary, his grandpa, George II, is in the cemetery plot with his two wives who happened to be Gary's grandmas, Gary's father's mother and his mother's mother. Grandma is in the same plot with her aunt and mother-in-law; they are the same woman, and Grandpa and Grandma are cousins. Gary's parents, Uncle Lawrence and Aunt Edith, were buried outside of Rush City, east of the Grant House. Uncle Lawrence was my mother's stepbrother. Grandma's parents and sister Maud Gottry are in the Birchwood Cemetery in Pine City.

Great Uncle Luther Harvey, his wife, Sarah; his son Ray Harvey and wife, Lucille; daughter Evelyn Hill; her husband, Lenny, Ray's grandson Frank Harvey were buried in Riverside Cemetery in Grantsburg.

## Family Conflict

My boy cousins, Roger and George and maybe Gary, to a certain extent, could play with friends or go on outings on Saturdays. We usually got a lot of company on weekends, so it was my job to clean the house and bake pies, cakes, and bread and such for the thundering herd we expected. I would turn on my country music station. If George was home, he would turn on that blasted rock and roll. When he would go outside again, I would turn on my country music station again. He'd come back in the house and turn the rock and roll on again. To this day, I dislike rock and roll; it brings back bad memories. I got in a lot of trouble for turning the country music on. I was the outside, and they considered me to be an interloper and scullery maid.

I never saw a group of people who were so unhappy in my life. I was happy when the iceman came because I knew we would get some ice chips that tasted good on a hot summer day. We had an icebox; he would bring a huge block of ice and chip off the ice until it fit in the icebox. Memories.

When the old timers would get together with their thrash machine and go from farm to farm, it was something to see. The last farm to thrash oats one year was the first the next year.

Silo filling was different; each farmer had his own, especially when corn choppers were used. In the early years, we didn't have a hay baler. We used a hay loader and slings. What a miserable duo that was. You'd put a sling on the hay rack, a good layer of hay, another sling, another good layer of hay, another sling, and another layer of hay. Then you were ready to unload the hay in the hay mow. The end of the slings had rings; the rings were attached to a hook that lifted the hay in the hay mow. You had to be careful that you got the right rings or you had a mess. Grandpa was on the tractor; he would pull the rope attached to the hay sling and pull the hay up into the mow. Then he would trip the sling, and we'd go back for the second sling, etc. If the thing would trip for some reason, then we would have to use the hay fork to get the hay on the mow.

## Lonely

I was a solitary kid when Uncle Lawrence and Aunt Edith and the boys moved to the other farm. I spent a lot of time in the woods with my books and picking berries when they were ripe. The first Zane Grey book I read was *The Light of Western Stars*. I said, "When I got a home of my own, I was going to have the complete set." I had no idea how many that was. Walter J. Black had a matched set; they cost $10 for four books. When I got twenty-four books, my husband told me to cancel, but I wouldn't. A month or so later, I got the rest of them all forty-five books. I paid them off like I did before, a total of sixty-nine books.

Today the price is higher for one book, and I got four books. He is my favorite Western author; he lived what he wrote about. I especially like the series *Betty Zane*, *The Spirit of the Border*, and *The Last Trail*. They are about Zane Grey's ancestor. Ebenezer Zane, Jonathan Zane, and Betty Zane were brothers and sister. Isaac Zane married an

Indian Princess. Lew Wetzel was the Spirit of the Border; the Indians called him death wind. He had such hatred for all Indians. They killed his parents, sisters, and baby brother. So he showed mercy to no Indians he found. He and Jonathan were friends. Jonathan was founder of the City of Zanesville, Ohio.

My son is a reader as I am. My daughter is not; she's like her father. I bought Dan a set of Hardy brothers' books and Dianne, a set of Nancy Drew. Both of my great-granddaughters love books; they are young yet. Angil is four; she looks at pictures and makes up stories about them. Melina is seventeen months, and she likes picture books too. I also think my granddaughter Donna, the girl's mother likes to read also. My grandson has other interests, so I don't know about him.

## Home Place

We lived 4 miles east of Rock Creek, a nice quiet neighborhood. Bud and Barb lived on one side of us and Allen and Doris Johnson on the other side of us. My great-great-grandfather owned the farm where Allen lived. His daughter Jane married George Stevens I. His son was Frank Harvey who was my great-grandfather. My great-grandpa Frank had one sister and one brother who died at a young age. Ida Harvey was twenty years old when she died on October 9, 1884, from diphtheria. She would be 146 years. Her brother died at the age of sixteen on October 12, 1884, also from diphtheria. He would be 142 years old. Their father buried them at midnight. He put them on top of a hill and marked the sites by planting two trees. Then he walked off the farm. I got our funeral director to make up tow markers for me. I put one by each tree. People were using the trees for deer hunting. Now they know they are grave sites.

Grandma was born in 1879, so Ida was fifteen years old when Grandma was born; Asa was eleven years old when Grandma was born. Grandma was not quite five years old when they died.

One Memorial Day, I was walking in the same area where I walked when I was a kid. I was inspired to write a poem about my ancestors. I call it "Back in Time."

# Back in Time

One day I took a notion,
To go back through the years,
To the place of my childhood,
A place that I hold dear.

I walked in the same old fields,
Among the same old trees,
The years seem to slip away,
Once again, I was a teen.

I'd take my book and a little,
Dish and to the woods I'd go,
I'd pick my berries and read my book,
At peace within my world.

I was searching for two siblings,
Who died many years ago,
I knew we were related,
But how I did not know.

I found them on top of a hill,
Beneath two lofty trees,
May God in His mercy,
Grant them eternal peace.

But fifty some years have come,
And gone, my hair is turning gray.
But for a while, I was a kid
Carefree, young, and gay.

I enjoyed writing the above poem. It brought such good memories of the good times I spent in the woods. I felt such peace there.

## Neighbors

Bill and Christine Broz lived east of Allen Johnson. They had two kids, Eugene and Sharon Broz. I think she died on March 1, 1958. Her dad would pay her $1.00 a mouse for each one she caught, but she kept catching the same dead mouse. I don't know how long that scheme lasted. Walter and Bertha Eng lived on the Rock Creek Road; their son Dennis got killed in a car crash several years ago. Frank and Mary Bible and their large family lived below the hill. The Bible family had twelve children. I knew several of the younger kids, Marian, Leroy, Kenny, Don, Verna, Lucille, and Rita; and the rest were older, a nice family. Doris Caroon and her parents, Bill and Ruth, lived on top of the hill. Whenever I go to Pine City on Highway 70, I drive past their house; it was moved. Holmes house, his wife, son Berl and daughter Jean were farther west on the Rock Creek Road. Otto Nimetz family, Richard Thieman family, Gordon Johnson family, Paul Mettling family, Clarence Christianson family, Louie Baum family, Tom Gay family, the Jacobson family, and the Gunnard Shoberg family all lived on the Rock Creek Road.

The old school house District 13 was about one-half mile from my home. Carl Johnson and his wife lived by Bud and Barb's place. Next to the school was the John Swenson family. The Swenson's kids I knew best was Ann, Floyd, Ray, Joy, Warren, and Lewis. Lucille died when she was young. Dean got killed in the service; the older kids, I didn't know.

Hjalmer and Beta Nelson were next, farther down the road. Charlie Rydlund lived next door to him. The Rudquist family lived on the neighboring farm.

Grandpa Stevens's first wife was Amanda Rydlund, sister of George and Charlie. George's wife was the sweetest person. They never seemed to have much, but every Christmas, I got a red Santa Claus sucker with white trim on it, cherry flavored. Charlie married Myrtle Rudquist; they had one daughter. I was always scared of Charlie. To me, he seemed different. George and Florence lived on the next road south of us. The East Rock Creek Baptist Church that I went to was on that road. Rodney Lindell, my old classmate, lived on that road. That lovely old church was where I went to Sunday school and Bible school in the summer. Rev. Cliff Holm was our pastor; he also made me think of a young Andy Griffith, tall and solidly built. He would play ball with us; we had a ball field south of the church. When we were baptized, we didn't have a baptizing thing, so we had to go to the Stanchfield Baptist Church. We were walked down stairway and into the water.

The Marty boys, Galen and Gordon, married the Anderson sisters, Lorraine and Margaret. The Hendrickson family raised bees and sold honey; still do, I believe. The Dahl family raised chickens and sold eggs. I can't remember everyone who went to that lovely little church. It broke my heart when someone turned it into a home. To me, that was God's house.

The Anderson brothers have a threshing party every year south of Rock Creek, off old Highway 61. He has a lot of antiques. When I was a young girl, he and his father had a portable sawmill. They went from place to place and sawed lumber. We called Mr. Anderson "Sawmill Anderson." He sawed our lumber before 1952 because Grandpa was alive then. He needed some more farmland, so he cut down one section of woods. So that's where the sawmill came in. I never saw a steam engine that big in my life. I wonder if it still runs. I bet it does.

## Meanderings

I drive by my old home once in a while. Not much has changed in the fifty-three years since I left there. The road is the same, no black top there; the road is like a washboard it can get awfully dusty when the road gets dry. Some of the older houses made way for newer homes. My creek is still there. The blackcap bushes and raspberries,

I hope, are still there. I took a walk in the creek, but it was dry. I remember when it had some water in it. The trees are somewhat bigger; we had some cedar trees. I would climb the trees. That was fun, but when the time came to come back down, it wasn't fun. When I picked berries, I never took any home. I would find a nice shady spot, sit under a tree, and eat the berries and read my Zane Grey book. That was my idea of heaven. It was solitude I treasured. We had several trees; we had several trees that I enjoyed climbing. Some of them, I was completely out of sight of. I would spend quite a bit of time up there. I'd go there to get away from Grandma. She never like to have me around to bother her, so I was content to be by myself. I am still the same way today. I spend quite a bit of time alone. I recharge my batteries that way, make peace with myself and connect with my heavenly Father. I spend quite a bit of time with my family, all four generations of us. It's me, my children, Dianne and Dan, born April 8, 1958 and December 21, 1964, my grand-children, Donna and Chucky, and my great-grandchildren Angil and Melina. They are the closest family members I have.

The closest in-laws I have are Marie Pistulka, Ruben's sister and her family, her son Randy and his wife, Danette; their children Jared and Rebecca and her daughter Charlotte Carey, her husband, Don; their children Jonathan and Amanda.

Marie Pistulka, my sister-in-law          Donna Shogren

## *Ruben Shogren*

It was in 1956 and my cousin Roger wanted me to meet a friend of his. I was busy and wasn't too interested in meeting anyone, but finally I told him okay. So on July 7, 1956, we had a blind date. It was Ruben, Marie, Roger, and I. I don't even know what we did or where we went. I do remember when we got back home and were visiting in the car. It was dark and we watched a man's barn burn down. We dated all summer and fall; and in December, we got engaged to be married. On May 24, 2957 we got married at the parsonage in Grantsburg, Wisconsin. We were married by Rev. Gordon Johnson, Baptist minister. I left Minnesota on May 28, 2957, after I graduated from high school. I was a farm girl most of my life, so that wasn't a great change for me. The change was the fact that as a solitary girl, I now joined a close-knit family of four—father, mother, brother, and sister. That family did everything together. When it came to picking berries, no one went until everyone could go. When it came to milking, gardening, haying, and other assorted activities, they included me; and I appreciated that. But I rebelled because I was used to being on my own and doing things by myself. I was like a square peg in round hole. It didn't work very well. I got into more trouble when I'd go off by myself and pick berries. Gradually, we worked it out.

Graduation Picture

Donna Shogren

My favorite job on both farms was silo work. I loved to hand the distributor pipes when we filled the silo with chopped corn. I'd make all kinds of big piles and then tramp it down. To me, that was fun. I also like the smell of silage. We had a Farmall F12 tractor. I was raking hay on the Iverson place on the bank of the St. Croix River. I was so short that my foot slipped off the clutch and jack-knifed the tractor and rake and killed the motor about a foot from the river bank. I told my husband I wouldn't sit on that tractor until he welded about an eight-inch piece of metal onto the clutch; it worked fine then. I liked working with the calves and milking cows on the Iverson place. We had an outside corral where we tied the cows and milked them. The biting flies liked that too. We raised chickens, ducks, cats, dogs, sandburs, cows, calves, horses, sheep, and goats—a typical farm but no pigs.

Ruben decided he was going to take a bunch of duck eggs and let a crabby old chicken hen hatch the eggs. She hatched them okay, but her babies found a water hole and decided to go in the water for a swim. We sure had an upset mama. She would wade out in the water up to her belly feathers, clucking away, but her babies stayed in the water until they wanted to get out. That was a dirty trick but an interesting one also.

My husband was wounded in Korea. He was working on a baler and a thunder storm came up suddenly. At the first clap of thunder, he was flat on his belly; it was a reaction to the time he was wounded in the Korean War.

In 1978, we had a big decision to make. They quit taking milk cans at Burnett Dairy. We would have to put in a bulk tank or quit. Our barn was getting old, and it wouldn't pass inspection. So we sold off most of our herd, kept a few older cows, and raised some young stock.

My father-in-law died on January 13, 1974, one day short of his eighty-third birthday. He was born January 14, 1891. He was a World War I vet. His name was Adolph Shogren; he had a gentle soul. If he got a sliver or a cut that needed tending, he would come to my house to get fixed up. My touch was more gentle than my mother-in-law's. My mother-in-law died on February 3, 1981. She was seventy-six. She was born July 23, 1904. Her name was Alice Shogren, a strong woman.

My father in-law was born in a log house, not far from Fish Lake, southwest of Grantsburg. Now it's called the Fish Lake Wild Life Area. His playmates were Indian children that camped on the banks of Fish Lake. They couldn't talk to each other, but they had fun anyway. Adolph had one older brother, Art Shogren.

Ruben was born on July 29, 1931, in the old Grantsburg hospital. At the time he was born, they lived south of County O. Marie was born May 26, 1936, in Sterling Township area. They moved 10 miles southwest of Grantsburg in 1940. In 2010, that was seventy years ago.

My in-laws always had a large garden. One fine summer day, I had my eye on a dandy watermelon. I decided I was going to take the watermelon and give it to my family for dessert. I picked that melon and took it to my kitchen. Imagine my shock and horror when I found out it was not a watermelon but Citron, the pale tasteless stuff that was cooked in syrup and added to fruit cakes. It was a painful lesson facing my in-laws and telling them what I did. We used to pick cucumbers for Gedneys. They had a pickle factory out by Grantsburg Lumber Company owned by the Fallstrom family. I remember pickling cucumbers. One day as I turned the vines to see the little cues, I walked up a huge gopher snake. Scared the living bejeebers out of me; they are harmless, but they look like a rattle snake to me. I don't like snakes in any kind or size. Urban Olson was the man who got us started. Hector Unseth was in charge of the pickle factory.

I remember picking potatoes at Emil Heineman's place; his wife was a sister of Aunt Sarah Harvey. It was hard finding all the potatoes because he had a potato digger and the potatoes would get covered up with dirt.

## Meals on Wheels

My mother-in-law had a stroke in 1978, so the county figured if she got involved with Meals on Wheels, she would take an interest in life again, especially if she saw a new person every day. They were

30

having trouble getting drivers, and they would have to quit. I wasn't working, and we sold most of our cows, so I said I would take the route. This was on Friday. I started the following Monday. I started in May 1978. I'm still doing it to this day. In 1980, they thought Ruben had cancer. Thank God he didn't, but it got me to thinking. I married right out of high school. We farmed, so I wasn't trained for anything. We paid into Social Security, but it went toward his but not mine. He got compensation from his war injuries, but if he died, so did his compensation. I had a chance to get certified as a CNA; in September 1981, I started CNA training. In November 1981, I started working at the Burnett General Hospital ECF. I worked there for fifteen years. My husband did the meal route during those years. I fell on the ice and hurt my shoulder in November 1996. I had to retire. I retired until the spring of 1997. I went back to delivering meals, splitting the route with my husband. I brought my daughter on board. By this time, Ruben was starting to lose his sight because of his battle with diabetes. He also had a start of Alzheimer's, and it was dangerous for him to drive a car. He broke his hip in 2000, so he was in the vet's hospital for several weeks. Dianne took over her dad's route. During the summer, she took her kids along with her. They are named Donna and Chucky. Now Donna's daughter Angil goes with her grandma and helps her. Angil is four years old. That makes four generations of meal deliverers. I'm proud of my family for doing what they are doing.

When Ruben got out of the hospital, they said he would be using a walker, but he was walking by himself. The first heart attack was at the senior center. He only had a small portion of his heart that was working. The doctors warned me that he could die suddenly with no warning. It was very stressful. I was living with a time bomb. You never knew when it would go off. On June 4, 2004, he had a fatal heart attack at home about 3:00 a.m. He died in his sleep. We were married for forty-seven years. I was alone again. On the first anniversary of his death, I wrote this poem.

# Ruben

Sometimes I get a little lonely
because I lost my mate,
but forty-seven years have come and gone
and most of them were great.

Sometimes we walked in the valley
sometimes we climbed the hill,
but we traveled that path together
life never broke our will.

But now our paths are divided
and I must walk alone,
until our paths join again
and Jesus leads us home.

I am proud of the poem that I wrote about Ruben. It's been six years since he died. I can't wish him back the way he was the last years of his life, but he's not worried about losing his sight or anything else.

I will be involved with meals for as long as my Father wants me to be. It's His decision. The people and the scenery and the routine is something I need badly. It keeps me centered and from getting depressed. I have been around elderly people my growing up years, so the work at ECF and Meals on Wheels was natural.

I drove for Bill and Violet Woodard, Elsie Hanson, Elsie Dahl, Gertrude Hammergren, Christine Shogren, Leander Beckstrom, Alice and Adolph Shogren, and others, so it was expected that I would do that kind of thing. I never actually worked with patients on a daily basis until I took care of an elderly couple for parts of two years, five months one year, and seven months another year. This couple had their share of problems. She had arthritis real bad and he had Multiple Sclerosis. They both died in 1981. He in April, and she died October 13 on her birthday.

I was almost forty-three when I started working for ECF. I worked for a short time at Grantsburg molded products. I made poker chips and other things. That and ECF was the only time I punched a time clock. I think why I was good at working with the elderly people is that I never let myself get too attached to them. I like people but never let them get too close to me. I lost so many people in my life; I wouldn't get too close to anyone because I didn't want to feel that sense of loss.

I had only worked there a few weeks when we lost our first resident. He called nurse, so I went to see what he needed. After I took care of his needs, I asked him if he needed anything else and he got a twinkle in his eye, and he said, "I could use a hug." I was in siren with Violet, and we stopped at a cafe for coffee. Ray Swedberg from Swedberg Funeral home told me had just picked up one of our people. He told me who it was. It was quite a shock. Ray's son Tim was one of my residents that was on my group at ECF, so he knew who I was.

I learned a painful lesson. One day I was transferring a lady from the wheelchair to the bed. I asked her if she could stand up. She said she could, so I stood her up, pushed the wheelchair away, and she sat on the floor. After that, I locked the chair until I had my patient sitting on the bed, and then I pushed the chair away; it was safer that way. I had one lady that liked her own nightgowns. She had a trapeze that helped her to get into bed, but she sat halfway between the feet of the bed. She said, "Dam, dam, dam." I was shocked. She informed me that wasn't swearing. A dam was something to hold the water back.

I asked a tall gentleman one day how tall he was; he told me he was five feet sixteen inches. The thing stuck in my mind was five feet since I'm about five feet nothing or so, and he towered over me. When I analyzed it, then it came out to be six feet four inches. I asked a lady how tall she was; she said she was five feet twelve inches. I enjoyed those people very much.

One of the most embarrassing things that happened to me was when I got stuck under a man's bed. The way that happened was the housekeepers would unplug the electric bed so they could move the bed and clean under it. They would forget to plug it in again. My resident was a big man. He would lie down and raise the head and the foot. It wouldn't work, so he would call me to plug it in. The plug in was under the mattress on the fame of the bed, so you would have to lie on your back and scoot under the bed. I am well-endowed in that area and other places as well, so I was getting pinched and stuck as well until I could plug the bed in, and I could get out. I made the mistake of telling Alice about that. Almost every time she saw me, she would call over and ask me if I was the one who got stuck under a man's bed. I think she lived to be 102 years. She was something else.

When my daughter got married in the spring of 1982, I told Tim who was about the same age as my son-in-law that I was going to adopt Tim because I only had one son and I need another one; but when Dianne married Sam, I didn't need to adopt Tim because I got my second son. Tim was in a car accident when he was sixteen years old. What a tragedy. Over the years, we've had some unique people. I remember I got a new lady on my group. I knew nothing about her. I got her ready for bed, sat her on the commode, and I got kicked on the shin by her artificial leg. I didn't know she had one. She lost her leg when she was a teenager. She told me her grandson told his friends how he could tap her knee with a hammer. One day he got the hammer; he forgot which leg was the artificial one, and he tapped her on her real leg. She ran him down, and I bet he wished he had an artificial butt. When I would do dentures and my people would get angry at me, I would ask them if they could whistle with no teeth. They would try to whistle and forget they were mad at me.

We had one man that thought it was funny when I squatted down to tie his shoes. He would push me, and I would land on my seat. One of my favorites was a native American gentleman. He had black wavy hair. I was collecting carousel horses at the time, and when he would get his hair cut, I told him I needed his hair for my carousel horses' manes and tails. I came to work after being off for a couple of days; his sister cut off his pretty hair. He saw me and pointed to his head. He laughed. I didn't get his hair. His mother was in the ECF when she died. I asked him if he wanted to see her. He nodded yes, so I took him to her room.

I had one lady who I usually put to bed second on my list, but something told me to put her to bed first. I got her ready for bed, did her cares, gave her water, got her settled down, put her side rails up, and then she took my hand, squeezed it, thanked me, let go of my hand, and she was gone. This is what I mean by instincts. That was the hand of God's work. I truly believe that. This happened quite a few times in the fifteen years I worked there. When I was giving my people baths was one of my favorite times of the day.

I like to make up little goofy songs. I used to sing Fraulein with Curtis; I made up one about Leander and Richard. It goes like this:

"Oh, rub a dub three people in the tub,
"Richard and Leander and me,
"I'll sit on the end, sink that tub
"And dump us in the sea."

We have had a lot of residents that are unforgettable. We had one lady; she was one of the first people to enter ECF. She came in 1970, I think. She had cerebral palsy. She was crippled, but she was the sweetest person. When she was a little kid, her dad made her a little cart that had wheels. She got around on that thing. She had a scar under her chin. She got going fast and ran into something and cut her chin. She had crippled hands, but she mad the prettiest things out of yam. Little Afghans. I don't have any idea how many she made, but they were beautiful. She used a loom with pegs; she'd loop the yam over the pegs and use a hook to knit the yam stitches. She was a marvel.

Another lady I will never forget came from Northfield, Minnesota. Her and her brother used to raise horses. I used to tease her about Jesse James when he tried to rob the Northfield Bank.

We had another lady who had twin babies, one girl and one boy. My husband worked for her brother for many years. When her twins were born, she was terrified of them. She asked her husband what they were going to do with them. He told her, "We're going to take care of them." That couple had a store in Trade River.

We had one lady that haunted me for years. I went into her room before I went home. I asked her if she needed anything. She said she was fine, so I went home. Her roommate told me she was crying softly. A while later, she passed away. If I had known, I would have punched out and stayed with her.

I always had trouble when I was filling the bathtub. I could never regulate the temperature of the water. I was okay. I had plenty of time to adjust the water in the tub. If it was too hot, add cold. If it was too cold, add hot. The problem I had was when rinsing the shampoo out. The water was too hot or too cold. I was always afraid of hot water, so I went more to the cooler side, less dangerous but more uncomfortable. I never did understand the complexity of bathtub water. I'd sing, "Oh, Lord, it's hard to be humble." To Tim, that was worth a small shove on the nose.

I remember Ruth. She and May Grace would play battleship. May Grace would call her Ruthie old girl. Ruth would tell me, "I don't know why she calls me that." Ruth lived to be over one hundred years old.

I remember Bill telling me if I wanted to lose weight to go on a vinegar diet. So I told him I bought a pint of pickled herring and I ate it. I asked him if that was enough vinegar. I recall Walter; he was a military man until he got MS.

In 1984, my son went into the navy. When Dan was on Westpac, whatever that was, I didn't hear from him for months. I didn't dare to show my concern to my husband because he was a wounded vet from the Korean War. Walter was my sounding board. One day he wasn't feeling well and I was talking nonstop. He said to me, "Don't you ever shut up."

I said to Walter, "If I have my mouth wired shut, I'd get rid of a few problems, eating, talking, and living. I had a real bad cold, stuffy nose, and all. If I had my mouth wired shut, I would get rid of my problem of living because I couldn't breathe through my nose." He was trying not to laugh, so I left for a while. And when I came back later, everything was okay again. Walter and his wife had four daughters. His third daughter would come and take her father out quite often. He was in a wheelchair. He was moved by the Hoyer lift. She also had a Hoyer lift to get him in and out of the vehicle. She handled him like an old pro. He was well over six feet tall. That experience with Walter taught me a whole lot about people. I learned to be more considerate of how a person was feeling. That was a very good lesson to learn.

Walter's mother was terrified of the Hoyer lift. So I made up a little song. "Tonight that Hoyer let me down, and I sat funny on the ground, the one good machine I thought I'd found, but tonight that Hoyer let me down." There was another verse, but you get the idea. She would ask me where she was, and I told her in bed. She asked how she got there, and I'd say by the Hoyer lift. She was so busy listening to that silly song that she forgot about being scared.

I remember when we got a waterbed mattress for one resident. Trying to move a person on that thing was something to behold. That was awful.

We had one lady that would crochet around berry boxes, the plastic ones. They were so pretty. She would make ornaments and dip them in a solution, and when they dried, they were rigid. She was an amazing person. She picked funny names for her children though. Her daughter's name was Arbutus. One son was Lindy, another son was named Ellsworth, and Robert was a common name. I can't recall any other children she had.

Another spicy lady we had told me one day that when her first baby was born, she was going to name him Riley Ethan, if it was a boy. He was and she did. She went some place and proudly showed her baby off. This older lady asked what the babies name was, so Ellen told her. The old said, "Huh, could have been called Gallagher." Ellen was so angry her eyes sparkled. Her son got killed in WWII, so he is buried in Europe.

We had another lady who was a direct descendant of Mr. Lewis of the Lewis and Clark expedition. This was on her mother's side of her family. Lewis and Clark were early explorers of the Western states. Her name was Mildred. Her husband was related to Casey Stengel. He had something to do with baseball, I believe.

We've had a large variety of people from all walks of life. We've had a dentist, chiropractor, and his wife, farmers and their wives, ministers—all kinds of people. The minister who married Ruben and me back in 1957, Gordon Johnson, was one of the residents I took care of. When Ruben and I had been married thirty plus years, I asked Gordon if he thought we'd make it that far. He told me, "I knew you'd make it." We made it to forty-seven years until he died. It was getting toward the end of Gordon's life. I went to work that day, and I went to his room to check on him. He was sitting on his bed. He patted the bed and asked me if I could talk to him for a bit. He was feeling down. And he told me, "I don't know what's going to happen."

My answer, "Gordon, you are in good hands."

He thanked me and he said, "I needed to hear that." I guess even ministers need a little positive reinforcement.

Every person I've had as a resident has added something to my life. Most of it has a positive effect on me. I've had a few who have a negative effect. I won't dwell on them.

Sarah told me about the day she saw "Big Gust Anderson." She was going into the drugstore for her father. They met that big guy in the doorway. She said she looked at those big feet, looked higher, higher, and higher until she saw his hat, and she burst into tears. He was about seven feet six inches tall. He used to be a marshal in Grantsburg. My father-in-law said he would pick up two normal-sized men by the scruff of the neck and carry them down the street into the jail cell. We have Big Gust days every June. We have a carved life size statue of Big Gust. He is a town treasure, our very own town hero. He's buried in the Riverside Cemetery. I imagine he still has descendants living in town. I don't think he ever married or had children so that direct line is gone.

We had one lady who did not like peas, especially pureed ones. I was feeding her on night at suppertime. I gave her some peas. She gave them back to me all over my uniform top. What a mess. I think she decided my top need a little more color.

I was making Ellen's bed one afternoon; I was squatting down by the bed. I had her sitting in her recliner. She said to me, "I wish I was over there. I'd kick you in the butt."

I answered her this way, "That's why you are over there and I'm over here." She had a quick wit. We've had brothers, also sisters, sister-in-laws, mother and son, and husbands and wives—almost every combination.

Viola was a nice lady we had at ECF. She sat down at the end of the hallway, so she could watch us CNAs when we came to work. At the end of the driveway, the street was very icy. When it got warm, the ice melted and water was running. Then we got quite a few inches of light fluffy snow. I started up the incline, slipped on the ice, and landed on my back in that fluffy snow. I had snow in my pockets, my purse, and all over. I just started laughing, lying on the snow bank. She said if I didn't move, she was going to send someone to haul me out of the snow. She was a nice lady.

In November 1996, I fell on the ice and damaged my left shoulder. I went to work that Saturday afternoon. I fell on Saturday morning. I couldn't lift my arm to undress my five-feet-sixteen-inch resident even when he sat down. I only did half my people that Saturday. I wrote out my resignation. I couldn't do my work, so I had no business being there. Here it is—2010—and my shoulder still bothers me at times. We had machines to help with lifting, but we had to walk our residents. And even with a belt around their waist, if they started to fall and I grabbed them, I did more damage to my shoulder. We could both be on the floor. I retired for the safety of my people. I hope in the fifteen years I worked there, I was able to bring a measure of happiness and comfort to the people I came in contact with. If I did, then I served the purpose that God intended me to do. I can only say I did my best to treat people with respect. We lost three hundred people in the fifteen years I worked there.

I retired for a few months, November 1996 until May 1997. That was enough of that. I resumed my original job of delivering Meals on Wheels.

Ruben's health was starting to fail, and the route was too long for one person. He would forget some people. I've been doing this job again for thirteen years. Dianne went with me, so I divided the money with her. In the near future, things were changing. It was getting dangerous for Ruben to drive a car. His diabetes was out of control. He was losing his eyesight. His blood sugar could be over five hundred at bedtime; and by three in the morning, it could be twenty-three. I put honey inside of his cheek, and his blood sugar would come up; and for a while, he was okay. In April 2000, he broke his hip, so he was in the vet's hospital for several weeks. When his driver's license came up for renewal, I let it expire. I didn't want him to drive. It was too dangerous. He wasn't happy about it, but I had to consider his safety and the safety of other drivers.

When Ruben and I got married in 1957, he had a black 1948 Ford car. It had a rounded back. It made me think of a turtle. He also had a Model A. In the fall, when we cut the corn, we put it in bundles. We took so many bundles, tied them together, and made corn shock; they were in the shape of a teepee. When the corn was dry, we would run it through a shredder to separate the ears from the stalks. The deer also liked the corn shocks. We would take the Model A and catch the deer with their heads in the shock eating the corn. We chased them away driving the old Model A car.

I remember in 1959. Dianne was fifteen months old and found a dandy patch of blueberries. Ruben said I couldn't take the '48 Ford to the woods to pick blueberries; I did anyway. I picked a couple of 5 quart ice cream pails of berries. Dianne was standing in the front seat. She reached for some berries and so did I. I took my eye off the trail I was on in the woods, and I ran into a tree. I took out the headlight. It took me a long time to live that one down. I wasn't going fast, so the light was the only damage I did. Many years later, I wrote a poem I called "Blu-bear-ies." I took my car out to the blueberry patch. I was in a wooded patch and something growled at me. I don't know if it was a bear or not, but I was glad I had my car.

We are getting so many bears in the country, and we also have them in town. I am glad I am on the second floor in my apartment. The poem goes like this.

# Blu-bear-ies

I had a conversation with,
a bear I didn't see,
I wanted to eat some berries,
but I didn't want him to eat me.

I don't know if he was around,
as I found my favorite treat,
wild delicious blueberries,
they are so good and sweet.

I told him I would pick a few,
but I'd leave the most to him,
berries are for sharing,
I told him with a grin.

So I picked a few berries,
and went merrily on my way,
if he will leave a few for me,
I'll come back another day.

We had quite a bit of land on the lower farm. It was swampy down there with several islands and a very good blueberry picking. We also cut a lot of hay down there. On the edge of the meadow in the mossy areas, berries grew very well. The most berries I picked was when Danny was about six years old and Dianne was about twelve years old. I picked 143 quarts. I sold enough to buy both kids snowmobile suits. They stayed warm that year and more besides. One day I decided to pick berries down there. I was walking around the island. I heard the most gosh awful racket. I flush up a flock of sandhill cranes. I guess they wanted berries too. I thought I surprised a bear.

Art and Christine lived on the farm where my father-in-law Adolph Shogren was born in 1891. Art was going to sell his cattle and machinery. The day of the auction, he died. He had a heart attack in the barn. That was April 1, 1965. Christine died in 1967. I think they had four children—Wesley, Evelyn, and Dorothy and Donald—who were twins. Both men have passed away, but both women are alive yet.

Wes was married but had no children. Evelyn never married; Donald married Lois Lundberg, and Dorothy married Clare Melin. They had eight children: Trudy, Kathy, Bob, Jim, Rick, Cristy, Donny, and Laurie.

Christine's sister Elise Dahl called me one day, and she wanted me to take her to the doctor in St. Croix Falls. I dropped her off at the clinic, and I went down town to run an errand. While going down the hill, my brakes went out on the car. I laid on the horn as I went through the stop sign. I was almost to the fire hall before I could stop. My hero husband came to my rescue. When I went to pick Elsie up, I found out she fell in the bathroom, so they X-rayed her knee, but nothing showed up. The more she walked, the crack in her knee got more visible. She was in a cast from her ankle to way above her knee. One day she called me, and she wanted to go pick blueberries up at Christine's. I asked her, "What if we saw a bear?"

Her answer, "I'll tell him to leave. I was here first." She was one determined lady. She sat on her back side and scooted all over that blueberry patch, cast and all. She didn't get many berries but we had fun. I remember she talked Benny into letting her have a car. This lady had arthritis in her hands so bad they were all crippled up. She drove from Cushing to Luck on a hilly curvy road about 70 miles an hour. I was never so scared in my life. I think that was a start of my gray hair.

In the '70s for a part of two years, I would go to their house, get them ready for the day, line up their meds, get them some food, go home, come back in the evening, get them ready for bed, settle them for the night, line up their meds, and go home. I did that for five months, seven days a week the first year. And the next year, I did it for seven months, seven days a week—except I took one day off to go to a funeral. Their son took that day. It was too dangerous for them to stay by themselves. There was always the danger of a forest fire. I locked them in at night, and they stayed locked in until I came back the next morning. I am glad I gave them a little more freedom for a few months anyway. They both died in 1981. Elsie died on her birthday, October 13.

Our son Danny was born on December 21, 1964. We brought him home on Christmas day. He was our present that year, a good one too. Diane was born on April 8, 1958. She was our Easter present, also a good one.

Ruben, his mother, and Danny took some lunch to my father-in-law. He was working on the lower farm. Danny got excited, and he said, "Doggy." It wasn't a dog; it was a bear. He was about a year and half. That was the first bear that I remember being in the area. There are a lot of bears now for some reason.

Ruben came home with a puppy. I think he was a beagle and pit bull. I don't know for sure. He was smooth haired and black-and-white. Danny followed that dog everywhere. We got a dusting of snow, so I followed the tracks, dog, and kid. I could hear Danny crying, but I couldn't find him. When I finally found him, he was in the refrigerator. I had taken the crispers out when I cleaned the fridge. It was a Leonard, and when the door shut, it latched. So he couldn't get out. We bought one that didn't have a latch. That sure scared me. I asked Danny this summer how he got stuck in there. He said he crawled in, stuck his fingers in a little opening, and shut the door. His sister told me how she would go for a ride in the clothes dryer. She would crawl in, push the switch, and go for a ride. Thank goodness she couldn't shut the door. I had no idea she was doing that.

I had a few close calls in my travels down life's highway. One when I lived in Cornell. We had a creek below our house. Most of the time, it was quite dry; but in the spring, it ran full. I would stand on the bank and watch tree branches and other stuff float by. If I would have fallen in, I think that would have been the end of me. Even then, I had a guardian angel with me. I remember Mrs. Shipley; she had a grandson about my age. She had a trapeze in her yard. I used to hang upside down and swing on that thing. I could have broken my neck if I would have fallen off.

When we lived in Cornell, we had neighbor. Her name was Florence Roth. She and her husband Leonard and her two kids Doreen and Eddie lived next door. Florence was a good friend of my mother. I think we spent more time in their house than our own. Eddie was a cute little red-haired boy, cute as a button. He was my first boyfriend. I was an old lady of five years old. I sure tried to impress him with my pretty turquoise crocheted dress my mom made for me, but she died before she finished it, so another friend finished it. It was a circle skirt. When I twirled around, it made a perfect circle. I still have the dress sixty-seven years after my mother's death. Veta Wilson was the friend who finished the dress. I was five years old when I had a picture taken in the dress. My daughter and granddaughter have had their pictures taken in the dress. On October 14, 2010, my greatest wish came true. All five females in four generations have had their picture taken with the dress. They are me, great-grandmother, Dianne, Grandmother, Donna, Mother, Angil and Melina, and my great-granddaughters. I kept the dress in a dark place so the color is as vivid as it was when it was new. It makes me feel close to my mother when I can handle something that she handled so many years ago.

I remember two different times I could have been in very deep trouble if my cousin hadn't pulled me out. The first dangerous thing I did was play in a bin full of oats. The harder I fought to get out, the deeper I got in the oats. If the bins were deep enough, you can smother to death. The oats crowd around you so tight, and you get so tired fighting that you could die. The second dangerous place was in a swampy area at the bottom of the hill that we liked to slide on. That area was so wet and the snow insulated it, so it didn't freeze. It was like quick sand. When I got off the sled, I would sink. I was up to my waist in that stuff. It just sucked me down. My cousins had a rope from the sled, so they pulled me out. I was a muddy mess. I wonder about that area if it has gotten worse over the years. I have no intention of finding out.

## More School Stories

When I started first grade in the old country school, we had eight first graders. Their names were Ann Swenson, Donna Magnussen (me), Joanne Anderson, Jacqueline Thieman, George Stevens, Wally Baum, Rodney Lindell, and Gerald Anderson.

45

I should have graduated in 1956, but I started school in one school then transferred to another school, so I had to take first grade over again. I got through in 1957.

In the seventh grade, the school district changed. We had our choice to stay in the country school or go to Pine City. My cousin George Stevens, Wally Baum, and I elected to stay in the country school. Most of the kids went to Pine City and Rush City. When George and I were in the ninth grade, the teacher wanted us to put on a two-person skit. It was fun and funny.

A few years later, the school closed. Floyd Swenson took the old school down. When my kids were young, I told them that was where I went to school. They would tease me about going to school in a hole in the ground.

At school, we had a nice swing set and a swing that had rings. I could swing for the longest time on that thing.

I can only recall one man teacher that we had. His name was Raymond Doyle. My memories of him are not my favorites. I don't remember if he taught at the country school until it closed.

When I went to high school, we had one hour per week for church school. That was on Wednesday. Pine City didn't have a Baptist church, so we went to the Methodist Church which was my mother's church, but I was baptized Baptist.

I remember the programs we put on, putting up the stage, decorations, practices, and memorizing lines. It seemed that every holiday that came along, we had something going on.

I remember the four *J*s. I called them in my mind: Joyce, Janice, Joanne, and John, the Hischer Kids. The Muellner kids, Annabel, Bernice, and Richard. From the Bible family, I used to get Verna to yodel; she was good. Sharon Broz was a honey. She and Marian Bible where classmates and friends. The Clarence Christianson kids: Gerald, Pamela, and Diane, I liked that cute little girl so much. I said if I ever had a girl, her name would be Dianne too.

I think Julia Christianson was a war bride and Clarence brought her to America. I remember hearing their son Gerald was born on the way to America somewhere on the Atlantic Ocean.

The Swenson family was large also. The ones I knew the best was Ann, Floyd, Ray, Joy, Lewis, Warren, and Dean; he got killed in World War II. Lucille died young. The rest of the family was older, so I didn't know them. I'm not an envious person ordinarily, but I did envy anyone with close family ties.

Arvid and Ebba Anderson had a large family also. Their kids' names were Charles, Wanda, Bill, Yvonne, Gerald, Joanne, and Pat. I regret that I never got up enough courage to tell Yvonne how sorry I was for bullying her. I was so mean to her. By the time I got my courage up, Joanne told me she had died. Someday I hope to see her, and I will make peace with her.

Lewis and Vila Baum lived on the Rock Creek Road. Their kids' names were Harold, Cecelia, Wally, and another son I don't remember. Paul and Mavis Mettling had a large family. Mavis was a Grantsburg girl. Her parents lived about 1 ¾ miles north of our farm.

Before George's voice changed, he and I sounded alike. Wally Baum called one day and asked if I wanted to go swimming. He thought I was George. After that every time he saw me he turned red as a beet. He got killed on Highway 70 in 1958; he was only 19 years old. His parents were having an auction and they were notified on that day of his death. It was quite a shock. I always liked Wally. He was a good guy. Enough of this for now, I'll come back if I recall anything else.

## More Meal Route People

I had one gentleman that detested liver and onions. I didn't know that, so I took his dinner to him. I told him what it was. He asked me if I knew what I was. I said no. He said, "You are a liver deliverer." He asked me if I knew what should happen to liver deliverers. I said no. He said we should have to eat it every day for a month, and if we had any leftover to sleep with it under the pillow. Needless to say, I never brought liver to him again. At Christmas, he furnished me with some rosettes, were they good. I have fond memories of him. He lived in the house where he was born. His niece and her husband built a beautiful home on a hill. He asked me if I thought Janet would trade houses with him. I told him he could ask her, but I wouldn't bank on it. I lost track of him, so I don't know where he is living now. I hope he is well; he was fun.

With a meal route, our numbers go up and down. Sometimes we have as many as fifty and as few as twenty-eight. Now it's around thirty-four. The number changes; we lose some to death, nursing homes, hospitals, or any number of reasons. We try to serve our purpose to the best of our ability. Dianne and I are a team. If I have trouble, she comes to my rescue; and if she has trouble, I go to her rescue. We both can count on my grandson Chuck; he works nights at the cheese factory in Alpha. We could call him if we need to after he gets home in the morning.

I was not a very good mother when my kids were growing up. The crazy way I was brought up. I didn't want them to go through what I did, so I raised them to be strong and depend on no one but themselves. The only time I was a good mother was when they were sick. That was when I showed them I loved them.

Dianne went through a lot of turmoil during her high school years. I think she hated me, and she had every right to do so. I wasn't there emotionally for her. That was my fault; my childhood lacked any kind of affection or stability, so I was emotionally starved myself. So I wasn't able to show strong feeling to my children.

The Shogrens were good people, but they weren't overly affectionate, never showed their feelings; they were just there. I never saw a sign of affection from my father-in-law toward his daughter or any from my mother-in-law toward her son. You just knew it was there.

I wanted to be part of that unit, but I still wanted to be apart from them when I needed to be. The poor family didn't know what they had in me. Ruben didn't either. Thank God he saw something in me worth saving and keeping. He got more than he bargained for, an emotional wreck. It took hitting rock bottom when I turned to wine, and I realized where I was headed. I knew I was in trouble. After I lost Dad in December 1970 and my brother Dick in May 1971, I went to the Methodist Church and sat staring at the cross and crying. Our pastor, Rev. James Know found me in there. He started talking to me, and I opened up and told him my problems. He just let me talk, and he counseled me; and for the first time, I found peace in my soul.

It took a long time, but I finally made peace with my grandmother. I sat at her grave and told her a lot of things. I forgave her for what she did to me, and I asked her to forgive me for things I said to her. When I got rid of the hatred I carried for so long, I discovered that God gave me the ability to write poetry, words, and music. I got four songs recorded, also some poems published. Overtime, I turned into a human being instead of the spiteful, angry shell I was before. Even now as I write this, God has His hand and His Spirit guiding me. For instance, I was taking meals to a family named Fox; they lived on Dove Lane, and there were hills and valleys. I was on a dirt road and came around a comer and up a hill, and I saw the dark green of the pines and lighter green of some other trees, hay fields turning green, and I wrote this little poem.

# Green

There are so many shades,
Of green everywhere you look.
Paintings by the Master,
He could fill a book.

That was the most peaceful road I found. Once in a while, if I want to find a tranquil place, I go on that road again. I don't know what happened to the Fox family. I hope they are well.

I was driving a little Ford tempo on my meal route when I was inspired to write this poem.

# Driving

When my time comes
To meet my Lord
I want to be driving
My little old Ford

I want to be doing
What I love the best
Feeding my people
Later I'll rest

This happens to me a lot. I can see something, and it will trip something in my head; and before long, I have a poem. I don't try to analyze it. I just accept it.

Grandma was not a person to visit back-and-forth with the neighbors. Mrs. Mettling and Mrs. House would bring berries, and Grandma would head for her bedroom and tell me to tell the ladies she was sick in bed. I hope God has forgiven me because I had to lie to them, but I had no choice in the matter if I wanted to avoid the wrath of Grandma. She never wanted company. I don't think any relatives were welcome either, but she had no choice; they came anyway.

I will say she loved her sons, her daughters-in-law, and she tolerated her daughter; and Aunt Edith, she criticized. Aunt Edith was the unhappiest person I ever met. Grandma was awful to her. My mother, according to Grandma, was the most perfect person. That's what I was brought up to believe. According to some letters I have, she was not a very nice person. She was spiteful and angry. According to my grandma, you could be a nasty person but the minute you

51

died, you became a perfect person who never did a bad thing in your life.

When Grandma died in September 1954, two of her five children had already died, my mother and Uncle Frank. My dad and Aunt Violet were alive at the time she died, but none of her kids or her son-in-law or daughter-in-law saw fit to mark her grave. Uncle Ralph came to Terry Hejny's funeral who got hit by a car and died as a young child. I asked Uncle Ralph if he knew where his mother's grave was; he said no. I showed him where her unmarked grave was. He didn't seem bothered by it. When I started working and I had some extra money, I marked her grave. None of the other grandkids seem to care either. I don't know what that says about her as a mother or a grandmother.

I found myself putting Mom so high on a pedestal no human could achieve it. When I found out she wasn't perfect, it almost destroyed me. I can hear Aunt Edith telling Grandma, "You better tell her the truth. When she finds out, it will destroy her." Grandma and Aunt Edith never told me, but my stepmother did after Dad died.

Aunt Edith was right; it got me drinking and I was heading down a road I didn't want to be on. I have too many drinkers on both sides of my family, and I recognized the road I was on. It took me about twenty years to get straightened out. I fight the problem with alcohol to this day. As long as I don't touch it, I'm okay; but if I take that first drink, I know what will happen. I refuse to go there. I put my faith and trust in God, so I'm okay. He's my Rock I stand on.

Alcohol is a curse in my family. So far, my kids and grandkids aren't hooked on it. Thank God. My dad, brothers, uncles, and cousins were drinkers. I don't know about the female members of my family, except for Aunt Marian; she used to yell at Uncle Ralph for drinking. After she died, he found her stash of booze bottles in the basement. She wouldn't go to the liquor store or to a bar, but she had it brought to her home. She worked at the Colony. It was a place that took care of severely handicapped infants, children, and others. Maybe that was the only way she could do that work. I don't know.

I had some of the best times with Grandma when we were alone, but they were few and far between. One time I recall was, if I was good, she would let me help her wash the old dishes that were in the curved glass china cabinet. I loved working with those old dishes. I had to be good and quiet and not cause her any problems.

When I was twelve years old, I was told by my grandma that it was my job to bake the bread, pies, cakes, rolls, and doughnuts. I liked to make raised doughnuts. I never liked making cookies; she did that. This was quite a shock because this was a woman who always told me it was easier for her to do the baking herself instead of trying to teach a kid. She never followed a recipe book; all the measurements were in her head. How in the world do you measure a dab of this or a dash of that? She made some of the best sour milk pancakes I ever tasted. I never did figure out how she made them. How much bread I made depended on how many loaves I had left over from the week before; it ranged from six to eight loaves. I had a large aluminum pan that was used for setting the bread only.

My cousins used to come from the cities, and we would play cards, five hundred, and also poker. I didn't bid very often, but I'd set the ones who did bid. After a while, I got banned from playing cards.

I had to fry bread dough; sometimes I put butter, cinnamon, and sugar on it. I'd fry up three or four loaves of bread, maybe even set up a new batch.

Grandpa's brother Charlie Stevens lived in Rock Creek. We'd set down to dinner, and Charlie and Myrtle would show up. We would cook dinner for three and those two would show up. We'd have to get up and fix some food for them. We would have dinner a half hour earlier, and here, they would show up again. Grandma swore they could smell food cooking four miles away.

When I was a young kid, we would visit Charlie and Myrtle when they lived in the old Mickelson place on County Road O, southwest of Grantsburg. Myrtle's mother lived with them. She would go upstairs and look out of the window. I was scared of her. I thought she was a witch. Then they moved to Rock Creek. Dianne was born in April 1958. I took her to show her off when she was a few months old. Mrs. Mickelson was a Norwegian lady who didn't understand English very well. Dianne wet her diaper, so I was going to change her. I mentioned about her being wet. Mrs. Mickelson got so excited. She thought I was mad at my baby and was going to drown her in the stock tank. Myrtle was laughing when I came back into the house; she told me what her mother said.

There were three Stevens boys—Ervin, George, and Charlie. Charlie and Myrtle were an odd couple, but they got along with each other just fine. Charlie had Albert with his first wife; her name was Ida, his cousin. He had Hiram, Dora, Margaret, and Vernon with Mary, his second wife. Mary died in the house where my in-laws lived when they moved to the farm southwest of Grantsburg. I don't know what year she died.

I was married to my husband for forty-seven years. We have two children, Dianne and Daniel; two grandchildren, Donna and Chucky; and two great-granddaughters, Angil, age four and Melina, seventeen months old; three great-grandsons, Cody, eight years old; Brandon, five years; and Billy, three years. I will be seventy-two years old in December. I will keep on doing my needle work even though I have arthritis in my hands; it seems help keep them limber. I have bum knees, but I am putting off surgery. I'm body is kind of dilapidated, but my mind is good so that is helpful.

In 2019, Angil is thirteen years
Melina, ten years
Cody is eight years
Brandon is five years
Billy is three years

My husband was so afraid of going blind, so I can't wish him back the way he was. The day before he died, he went to Bob Johnson's funeral. Dave Edling told me he kept an eye on Ruben. He thought he was going to expire at the funeral. He died about 3:00 a.m. On the first anniversary of his death, I wrote this poem.

# Ruben

Sometimes I get a little lonely,
because I lost my mate,
but forty-seven years have come and gone,
and most of them were great,

sometimes we walked in the valley,
sometimes we climbed the hill,
but we traveled that path together,
life never broke our will,

but now our paths are divided,
and I must walk alone,
until our paths join again,
and Jesus leads us home.

I have an interesting memory of our school bus driver. His name was Bob Thiry. Our bus route went to the St. Croix River. We tried to get Bob to take us across the bridge into the State of Wisconsin. We thought it would be fun to cross the bridge. Bob finally had all he could take, and he said, "If you think I'm taking a bunch of minor girls across that bridge, you've got another thing coming." It never crossed my mind that it was illegal.

I've heard the old saying, "He's got lead in his britches." I don't have that, but I got some on my hands when I was in ninth or tenth grade. Ann and I were playing with a pencil. I made a grab for it; she tried to keep it from me. I got hit on the palm of my hand. After all these years, it's still there. That was in 1954 or 1955.

DONNA SHOGREN

Marie and Bob Wagenius were the ones that stood up with us. Ann was there too. Bob and Ann have been married for fifty years. Bob and his older brother Dennis were friends of Rubens for many years. Ann and I started the first grade together. Most of the Swenson family lives in Oregon and other Western states. Joy Brown lived in Minnesota. The Wagenius and Swenson families were good people as were my in-laws. I was proud to be in that solid family. I was kind of a rebel, but as I got older, I appreciated them more. They put up with a lot from me. I was not the best person to be around.

When I was growing up, I had two special strong women I really looked up to. Aunt Eunice was one. When they would come to visit us from Cornell, she would help with the baking and cleaning the house. They had seven children. Six of them were older than me. Only Helen was younger. Aunt Eunice told me she would have liked to adopt me, but having seven kids to raise during the depression, they had their hands full without adding one more. I think I only had four cousins younger than me. All the rest were older.

The second one was Aunt Marie. She was the wife of my mother's stepbrother Len Stevens. It is quite a jumbled family. For instance, I had an awful time trying to figure out how a person's aunt could become your mother-in-law. You did it by marrying the son of your dad's sister, her cousin. I always looked up to Aunt Marie. When she died, I went over to the funeral home in Pine City. She had written her autobiography. I was looking at the book, and I found a paragraph she had written about my brother Neil and me. I was so flattered that she thought enough of us to put us in her book. As I read it, I realized just how much she resented us and blamed us for preventing her son Ray from having a close relationship with his grandpa. She said Ray didn't play with us because we were *funny*. That revelation cut worse than a knife. I did something that day that I thought I would never do. I was so hurt and outraged that I stole a cucumber. Melon Vine Farm made up a small basket of veggies and put it on the floor by the casket. After I read that paragraph, I walked up to that basket took a cuke out of it and I left. I had intended to go to the funeral, but I couldn't force myself to go. I thought I would say something to Myrna and to Ray. I may be a lot of things, but being a hypocrite is not one of them. Oh, by the way, I ate the cuke when I got home. It sure tasted good. I haven't seen Ray and Myrna or Ray and Donna since that time.

Our family was broken up. Neil and I had no say in the matter. That decision was made by the grownups in our family. We were just transferred; we were probably five and six at the time. She was way out of line when she blamed us. I had a hard time forgiving her. I don't know when she wrote her book, but I certainly was not happy with her. She said the curved glass china cabinet Grandma had at the farm belonged to her and Uncle Len. They got it as a wedding present. I don't know if that was true or not. They got the secretary, book case combination, and made it in to a gun cabinet.

Uncle Lawrence gave the China cabinet to Dorothy when he left the farm and moved to Rock Creek. He left the house partly furnished, dishes, beds, and appliances. I bought a large kitchen cupboard, a dresser, and a bed. Several years later, Bud and Barb saw me at the grocery store.

Bud tore down the house, and he found my grandparents' wedding announcement. It told when they got married, it was 1900. Also it told where and by whom. I had it framed. It is just beautiful. That was my Grandpa and Grandma Rose. I also have Grandpa Rose's little Bible. Dad had that in his wooden box that I inherited.

## Cats and More Cats

We had a lot of different cats on the farm. In 1990, I had gallbladder surgery. I was sitting in the yard feeling sorry for myself. I was watching the kittens and the older cats playing, so I wrote this poem.

# Kittens

I love to watch little kittens
when they are at play
they take life the way they find
of each and every day

They run and jump and climb
some trees as happy as can be
I wonder If I could get a
cat to change places with me

The more I watched them, the better I felt. The only drawback I would have if I were a cat, I would have to eat a mouse, no deal, but God bless the furry friends He sent to help us.

Grandma would never allow any cats in our house. But on Sunday, we had company; she would never clear the table and wash dishes until the company left. So we went out to the care with our company. When they left, we went back in the house. We were not away; a cat sneaked in the house. The cat was sitting on the table eating the butter. Grandma got the broom, and I think that cat used up three of its nine lives by the time it got outside. We had one animal. I wouldn't call it a pet exactly. It was a bull. Grandpa would never keep a bull past two years. After that, he said they were dangerous. Duke had a ring in his nose. I used to snap a snap to his ring and lead him all over the place, picked him in one place until the grass got short, and then I'd put him somewhere else. I wasn't afraid of him, but I respected him. I was aware of what he could do if I let my guard down. We also raised pigs. We had a nice pen for them. One little guy was always getting out. I chased him until I was exhausted. Finally I went to get my cousin to help me round him up. While I was gone, he went back in the pen himself. I could never figure out where he got in.

We had a corn crib not far from the chicken house. We took an old bed spring and put it at the end of the corn crib. We would hang onto the window frame on the corn crib and jump on the bed springs. That was our version of a trampoline. After a while, we got real good at it. We went quite high.

I remember hearing about when Grandpa got bit by an old sow. She had given birth to a bunch of piglets. Grandpa reached into the pen for some reason. She bit him; her teeth went right through the palm of his hand. He was lucky she didn't hit any bones, but they worried about infection, but he was okay. Sows were unpredictable, especially when they had young babies. Their large size made them a force to be feared. I think all babies are sweet and I enjoy them, but baby pigs are just adorable.

I had a very nice lady named Karin on my meal route. Karin came to Trade Lake to live with her daughter Nyla when her health began to fail. Karin was a talented lady. She could do so many things. She made a rabbit when Nyla was a child. I think that rabbit was four feet tall or so. She had a beautiful white long-haired cat she named Angela. I would take Karin's meal to her, and I had a little game I played with Angela. So I wrote a poem about it.

# Angela

Karin has lovely cat,
Angela is her name.
I sure like that pretty cat,
We play a little game.

I asked her if I could scratch,
Her tummy, what do you think of that?
She thinks a while, then suddenly,
She lands flat on her back.

She seems so contented as,
I gently rub her down.
She seems so satisfied but,
She has a little frown.

She knows I have to leave her,
To complete my little route.
Until I see her once again,
I guess she'll have to pout.

We lost Karin a while ago. If Angela is still alive, I know she has a good home with Nyla. Karin came from Albert Lea, Minnesota.

Karin told a humorous story about when her kids Gary and Nyla were small. They were going by train from Chicago to Ohio. Nyla was nice and quiet, but Gary was all over the train. When they went through Indiana and the conductor yelled "Gary," he was announcing the train was going through the city of Gary Indiana. He was not hollering at Gary. Karin said he stayed in his seat for the rest of the trip.

## Fluid Drive Animals

Many, many years ago, I went to these ladies' house. I think I had my egg route at the time, and it had to be in the early '60s. My son was born in 1964, and she made me a baby quilt for him. I rapped on her door; she told me to come in, and when I did, I got the worst shock in my whole life. I was looking eyeball to eyeball with a skunk. It had been deodorized, but that was one animal I never expected to see.

Speaking of skunks, I had another encounter with one. This was in the wild, and it had its whole fluid drive intact. It was a beautiful January day, warm and sunny. We had a lot of snow, so I parked my car off the road and carried the dinner up to the house. Two bachelor brothers lived there. The house was to the left; the bam was to the right. As I walked toward the bam, a skunk came out of the bam and started toward me. I stopped and so did he. Then he turned around and hurried back to the bam again. I don't know if he smelled the dinner and decided to investigate or if he smelled the dinner and didn't like it and ran away. I don't know which I like the best. I know it was three months before we had that dinner again. It was sauerkraut and polish sausage; quite exciting. Bev always put some brown sugar in her sauerkraut. Sure tasted good too.

## Pets Galore

Once in a while, something comical happens. We had a lot of different pets on the farm. Two pets come to mind, Princess and Patches. Princess was a small dog, breed unknown, but she had a sense of humor. She would lay her front half on the ground, stick her butt up in the air, and tease the cat. Patches was a beautiful long-haired white cat, except she looked like someone had taken a paintbrush and put different colors of paint on her; hence, the name Patches. Princess would tease her, and soon, they were off: the cat chasing the dog. It never worked the other way. Patches would not be intimidated by the dog. I really enjoyed those two; they furnished a great deal of enjoyment. I have a lot of fond memories of the pets we had. Pal was a Pyrenees, and Collie, a huge dog. Lassie was a good cattle dog. Other pals were a cockapoo, Snoopy, a Chihuahua; Midget, a corgi; and Lassie or Goldie was a golden Lab, a beautiful animal. Shep was part coyote. It showed toward the end of his life; he got ugly. Here is a poem I wrote about them.

# Princess and Patches

Princess and Patches are,
really quite a sight,
when they play together,
it fills me with delight.

Princess is a little dog,
she weighs about ten pounds,
but in her heart, I do believe,
she thinks she is a hound.

Patches is a pretty cat,
as prim as she can be,
but I believe that in her heart,
she is full of dignity.

Patches is mostly white,
with long and silky fur,
With patches of different colors,
she's pretty that's for sure.

Princess likes to play with her,
she runs to and fro,
poor Patches looks so puzzled,
she don't know which way to go.

Together, those pets are something,
apart they are alone,
they both make me happy,
they are welcome at my home.

A lot has changed in the last few years; I gave princess to Dianne and Sam. Princess went to doggy heaven. Patches moved up to Dianne and Sam's with her kittens. I moved to town to take care of my great-granddaughter Angil; she is four years old.

Skog Road, I have traveled on that road more times than I can count. I suddenly became aware of a lone tree in a field. In the fall, it loses its leaves. In the spring, it gets a new coat. I wrote a poem about it.

# Lonely Tree

I saw a great big oak tree,
standing in a field,
in total isolation,
I wonder how it feels.

I wonder about its family,
and where it came from,
I bet its roots run awfully deep,
but now it's the only one.

It must get lonely,
standing all alone,
but maybe a bunch of birds,
call the tree its home.

But when it gets a brand-new,
coat as it does each spring,
its life will be renewed,
and become a lovely thing.

This year, it's hard to see the trunk of the tree; it is in a cornfield.
The corn is tall, so you can only see the branches and a little bit of
the trunk. The leaves have fallen off, so it's lost its coat, but it's still a
stately tree. I go past that tree quite often.

## *Raccoons*

I had a battle with a pesky raccoon. A few years ago, that animal was stealing our bird feed and wrecking our feeders. I decided to catch Rocky in a live trap. Our trap was too small. Rocky ran off with it. I rented a bigger one from the DNR. Rocky ran off with that too, so I had to tie it to a post. I wrote a poem called 'The Sage of Rocky and Me.' Here's how it goes.

# The Sage of Rocky and Me

I went to tell a story
a very touching tale,
about me and Rocky one of
us was bound to fail.

Rock is a raccoon as
persistent as can be,
but I was just as determined
so it was Rocky or me.

Everything I came up with
he beat me every time,
then I got the big guns out
I hope victory will be mine.

This story is not over
it hasn't come to an end,
and if he defeats me
I wish he could be my friend.

The battle is not over
the war has just begun,
there can only be one winner
I intend to be the one.

He ran off with the big trap
I tied it to a pole,
now it's in his ball park
that raccoon is no one's fool.

I bet he is laughing
as happy as can be,
at that interfering cat
and bumbling old me.

My pursuit of that raccoon
so far has come to naught,
it's outfoxed me at every turn
a rough battle I have fought.

But I am determined its
got to be me or him.
But my chance of catching
him, I think, is mighty slim.

Maybe it's a mama trying
to feed her brood
I guess I can't blame her
for trying to get some food.

I can't afford to feed her
and her whole family,
in-laws and outlaws and
everything in between.

Now my Norwegian dander's up
I'm looking for a fight,
but I'm going to try to catch him
when I set the trap tonight.

I hope I have finally scared
that raccoon away,
I haven't seen him now
for a couple of days.

But I'll keep the trap a little
longer maybe a day or two,
then if I don't catch the twerp
this story will be through.

I guess I am happy
Rocky's running free,
I got out foxed by a raccoon
but that's all right with me.

But I guess I am a winner he's
not stealing from our feathered friends
and if we don't tangle again
this story has come to an end.

## Meals on Wheels Again

Thirty-two years ago, when I got involved with the meals program, the thought came to me of the lady who got me started. Her name was Norma. Years later, I took meals to her. We came full circle. Who knows? Maybe someday someone will bring dinners to me. I hope when I can no longer serve in that capacity, someone else will; we will see. The route will be too much for one person to do by themselves.

I've had some of the same people on both services I've provided at Extended Care Facility and Meals on Wheels. First I've taken meals to them, and if they ended up at ECF, I have taken care of them there. Several people come to mind. Over the years, we've found a few people that have had strokes and also a few that have expired.

One sweet old lady comes to mind. I walked in her house with her dinner. I went past her bedroom. I saw her on her bed. I told her that dinner was here. She didn't respond, so I took her dinner to the kitchen. I walked back to her bedroom door again. I talked to her, no response. So I checked on her, and she had died.

Her dog, a chocolate Lab would jump up on the bed. He would come back to me then go back to her and back to me; the poor dog knew something was wrong.

I called 911, and I had to wait until the police got there. Her son told me he was glad he didn't find her. I really miss her but that all part of life; her suffering is over.

I was at the senior center one morning; I heard a lady mention homemade root beer. It brought back memories of Eileen, a lady we had at ECF. Many years ago, she decided to make some root beer. The warmest room in her house was the bedroom. So she stored it under the bed. Late one night, she heard popping noises. She thought someone was shooting in the house. It was the root beer popping the caps off the bottles. She said it was a sticky mess and ruined the mattress.

We had one lady that Dianne and I took meals to. It was on Thursday, and I didn't realize the next day was Good Friday and we would be closed for the Easter holiday. So Friday morning, I called Roger and told him we were closed on Friday. He said that was okay because Ann died at bedtime on Thursday. I wrote one of the most lovely poems, and I put it in a card for Roger and their son. I also took meals to his second wife and also to his mother.

# My Final Wish

When my life is over and
It's time for me to leave,
I want to go with dignity
I don't want anyone to grieve.

Jesus will be there to greet me
And hold me in His arms,
He'll tell me that He loves me
And we'll be safe and warm.

So don't be unhappy when
It's time for me to leave,
I'll come back to visit
I'll be riding on the breeze.

So when you go out walking
And you feel the gentle breeze,
It's my spirit that you're feeling
May it give you lasting peace.

The last several years, I have been taking meals to Adeline. She lived out by the Wood Lake Baptist Camp. Adeline's son is Roger, the one I mentioned in the previous story. I took dinners to his two wives.

I also took dinner to another lady at Courtyard Square. She was related to Adeline. The lady at Courtyard Square was named Naomi. I miss all of these special people. Adeline and Naomi, I believe, were in their nineties.

Courtyard Square got its name from the fact that it's on the site where the courthouse and jail stood. Grantsburg used to be the county seat. It had been from the time of its founding until the powers that be decided it should be moved to a more centered location. Grantsburg has the only hospital in Burnett County, the great Burnett Medical Center. The old hospital was built in 1930. My husband was born there in July 1931, and our daughter was born there in 1958. My son was born in the new hospital in December 1964. For a time, the old hospital was used as a nursing home until the new hospital and nursing home was built. The old hospital was then used for the village offices. The basement was where Meals on Wheels got started. The village offices went to the old high school after the new high school was built. Meals moved to the senior center, which used to be the old movie theater. Now the old hospital is an apartment building. I think it has several apartments. It's good that some of the old brick buildings have a second and sometimes more chances to be used again.

Grantsburg has quite a history. I think it was founded in the 1860s. We have the only hospital in Burnett County and the Dairy Coop in Alpha, 7 miles east of Grantsburg. The Dairy's cheese is sold worldwide. We have Crex Meadows and the Fish Lake Wildlife Area; this is home to all kinds of wildlife. We have bear, deer, sandburs, geese, ducks, and sandhill cranes. So many of God's creatures find a home here, and that includes me. I have been here for fifty-three years myself. I moved here as a bride; even though I am a widow, I still feel at home here.

This next section is painful to write for several reasons. The first reason is the things Grandma told me about Mom and Dad, both positive and negative are all messed up.

I was taught from a little girl that my mother was the perfect one. I put her so high on a pedestal that no human could live up to that.

According to Grandma, Dad was unfaithful to Mom. I don't know if that was true or not. I do remember plainly being taken by Dad to this place. They would sit me at the kitchen table, give me bread and butter and a glass of milk, and they would go upstairs. I can see that plainly in my mind. When I finished my snack, I would go outside to the bam, wander around, and finally go lock myself in the car and go to sleep. When Dad would come outside, we would leave. Her name was Mable Cole; her husband's name was Louie. I don't remember Louie at all. When this happened, I don't know if this took place before or after my mother's death. I have no way of knowing. Anybody who would know is no longer alive. The only way Grandma would know is if my mother was still alive, but I was only four. So I was quite young. My uncles were still alive, so maybe they told Grandma. I just don't know.

Mom wasn't so innocent either. I was told by my second step-mother, Ellen, that my brother Neil didn't belong to Dad. He came home and found her with another man. Ellen took great delight in telling me. This was after Dad had died.

Earlier Aunt Edith told Grandma that she should tell me the truth. She said if I found out, it would destroy me, and for a while, it almost did. I confronted Aunt Eunice when she came over for Fred McCann's funeral; they were related. I asked her if it was true, and she confirmed it. But she said a funeral was no place to discuss it, but she would tell me who Neil's father was. The next time I got to Cornell was to Aunt Eunice's funeral. No matter his paternity, Neil was my brother. My stubbornness caused a breach in our family for twenty-five years. I finally got it through my thick head that was stupid. So in 2000, I found him; he was in Joplin Missouri. For the next three years, we were brother and sister again. He visited us in Wisconsin, and I visited him in Missouri. We visited on the phone back-and-forth. Forgiveness is sweet. He died in December 2003.

I have letters that my mom wrote to her sister. She was down-right nasty in them. Also letters Aunt Edit wrote to Mom and letters Grandma wrote to Mom. Three of the most vindictive females I ever met. My granddaughter reminds me of those three.

I felt such guilt and despair at the way I treated Dad in favor of my mother. I found out I worshipped the wrong parent. By that time, they were both dead. I have to accept the fact that both parents were human and both were capable of making mistakes. One was no better than the other. I like it that way. In my mind, they are equal. I finally feel at peace with the thoughts of Mom and Dad.

I wrote about these episodes not because I want to expose dirty laundry, but it goes to show how adults can really mess up a little kid's life. This was part of my childhood. I had nothing to do with it. I had no control. My destiny was determined by my relatives and whoever had custody of me.

After I got married, it was another kind of life. The next twenty-one years, we farmed, milked cows, raised chickens, and raised two kids. I was the person several people called when they needed a ride somewhere. I drove for Mrs. Hammergren for eight years and the Woodards for I don't know how long. So I kept busy those years. I liked silo work and to plow land; my furrows weren't very straight. I tended to daydream when I was driving a tractor.

The year I turned forty-two, I started to gain control of me. Now I've put Christ, my Savior, in first place. I'm perfectly content to take second place behind him.

Before I made peace with Grandma, I couldn't write at all. When I wrote "Family Reunion," the words I wanted to write about my oldest brother wouldn't come. I told God after I wrote the first two lines that I was stuck. I said, "Father, it's your turn. I can't do anymore." He put the last two lines in my head. I had my verse. Thank you, God.

I'm going to sum up my life in a nutshell. I'm a mom, grandma, great-grandma, a sister-in-law, aunt, and great-aunt. I'm no longer a wife, daughter, sister, niece, or a granddaughter—that about sums up my life. I like being with my daughter and my son when he comes from the city where he lives. The other two members of our family are Sammy and Norman. Sammy is my son-in-law. He teases me about my mother-in-law's status. He has a good heart though. Norman is my grandson-in-law; he's married to my granddaughter Donna. He's a good guy. The other potential member of our clan is Chucky's sweetie, Kristin. She's a keeper, but we will wait and see.

Dianne and I do a lot of things together. We like to go shopping, and we take Angil with us sometimes. I would like to explain about Angil. She was born on Good Friday in 2006, so her parents named her Angil, and she is well-named. We also take Donna and

Norman shopping with us quite often and Chuck too when he is available.

I don't have any close friends. I like people, but I don't let anyone get close to me. I have an issue with trust. I never learn to trust anyone as a child so that carried over into adulthood. At times, I like being alone. I'm comfortable in that role. It recharges me, and I need that. The lack of trust as a child caused me trouble in school. During grade school, I was a bully. I wanted to belong in a group, but I didn't trust anyone—and being a bully didn't help my image. By the time I got to the upper grades, I outgrew my disruptive way. Thank God for that.

I'm faithful when it comes to something I believe in. It started with my forty-seven years of marriage, the thirty-two years since I got involved with Meal on Wheels and my fifteen-year career as a CNA.

During the time I was a CNA, Ruben did the meal route. In 1997, I started the meal route again. Ruben and I split it. Dianne went with me on my route, and then when Ruben retired in 2000, Dianne took his route. During the summer, Dianne's two kids joined in. She now has her granddaughter Angil, four, going with her so that is four generations of meal deliverers. I will do my route for as long as I am able, or I run out of people. I get inspired by the people I serve. I wrote the following poem. It is called "The End."

# The End

When it's time for me to die
I hope I'm in my bed,
Listening to the voice of God
His message in my head.

He's telling me to have no fear
when it's time to say goodbye,
I know my God is by my side
and it's my time to fly.

I'm listening to the angels sing
the wings in the dancing leaves,
I'm listening for the voice of God
and my soul's found lasting peace.

# Whispering

God is whispering
In my ear,
If I listen closely
The message is clear.

"Repent, My children
"Before it's too late,
"Then I will be there
"To open the gate."

"You are welcome in heaven
"Forever to dwell,
"In peace and happiness
"What a story to tell."

The birds are singing constantly
On this breezy Friday morn,
It's cloudy and dreary
But the rest is yet to form.

# Fred

The morning is crisp and sunny
I'm snuggled in my bed,
but I never get lonely
because I have my Fred.

Fred never argues or
tells me what to do,
he's always meek and mild
I'll keep him, the fact is true.

I never have to feed him
he's contented as can be,
he is a special guy and
I think I'll tell you why.

Fred is a monkey; he's
about a foot high,
he has a funny smile
and a twinkle in his eye.

Fred is a gorilla Dianne got out of a
claw machine at Walmart; she got
him for Angil, but I borrowed him
for a while.

# Writing

My journal's like a second skin
it's with me all the time,
when I get the urge to write
that idea is really fine.

The words go around inside my head
there's only one thing to do,
get out my pen and journal
and see the writing through.

Sometimes it's downright silly
sometimes the thoughts are deep,
I need to put it down on paper
if I hope to get some sleep.

Writing poetry makes me feel good; it gives me a sense of peace. If I'm writing something and I become stuck and can't find a word, I ask for Jesus's help. And soon, I'm unstuck. It happens quite often to me.

# The Country Choir

I have a country choir; they
start at the break of dawn,
at six o'clock in the morning
their voices are going strong.

A few are soprano; I hear
a bass that's swell,
I detect a sweet alto and
maybe a tenor as well.

Together, they are a mixture
a blended vocal choir,
they sing for long time
I hope they never retire.

But soon the choir is over
and they go about their day,
doing what birds normally do
living the typical way.

I thank them for their music
and God for the lowly bird,
they trust Him completely
and listen to His Word.

But now the bird choir
is starting to fade away,
I guess it's time for breakfast
I wish them a wonderful day.

Now that it's the twenty-fourth of October
I think the choir has gone south,
I don't hear theme now, so the
summer birds have found a warmer
place; I hope they had a good flight.

# Trouble

I know my Jesus
is watching my back,
I trust Him completely
and that is a fact.

He watches over me
when I'm on my route,
He loves me totally
there is no doubt.

When I have trouble
it's somewhere safe,
it happened today
at a nice lady's place.

My Father tells me
what I should do,
I'll follow His teaching
my whole life through.

I listen to Him when I
find something wrong,
sometimes I feel helpless
but Jesus is strong.

The temp light alerted me
that something was wrong,
I'm glad I paid attention
I will all day long.

So thank You, Jesus
I owe you so much,
I'll listen, Father
I long for Your touch.

This poem came about when I had taken dinner to Evelyn Wilson. I got ready to go, and I noticed my temp light was on. Her son came to my rescue; my coolant was a little low. Thank you, Warren, for helping me out.

# Who Am I?

I'm not the worst
and I'm not the best,
I've studied the lesson
But I failed the test.

I've tried my best
to do what is right,
sometimes I did it
I hope in God's sight.

I've tried daily to
help people along,
the ones who are weak
but also the strong.

I'll try to work until
my life is through,
delivering meals
faithful and true.

This poem came about when I decided to analyze myself. I discovered that because my childhood wasn't *normal*. I couldn't change that, but my present life could change; and with God's help and guidance, it did. I couldn't do it by myself, but God changed me. I looked at myself, and I thought, *You are a pretty good ole gal compared to the old me who's main goal was to get even with everyone around me.* It never did work. Thank God for that.

Here is a series of things that I marvel at. We have so many things to be grateful for. The main one, a Heavenly Father who loves and treasures us.

# I Marvel...

I marvel at the innocence
of a baby's smile,
I marvel at the beauty
of a country mile.

I marvel at the serenity
of a country lane,
I marvel at the nerve
that keeps a city person sane.

I marvel at the sight
of a baby bird,
he makes his parents understand
and he cannot say a word.

I marvel at the baby sheep
each one looks the same,
but Mom can tell each one apart
I wonder if they have a name.

I marvel at the gentle rain
as it falls from the sky,
we should accept the blessed rain
and never questions why.

I marvel at small children
and the sweet things they can do,
they're innocent and trusting
I hope their whole life through.

I marvel at the old folks
that have lived many years,
heal their hurts, dear Father
and wipe away their tears.

I marvel at the caring a mother
animal shows to her young,
she loves them the way they are
to watch them is a lot of fun.

I marvel at our Savior and
the tender loving care,
that He shows us daily, His
love He gladly shares. Amen.

I marvel at my daughter
the many things she can do,
she and her family have also
been tried and tried and true.

I marvel at my son Daniel
what a joy he's been to me,
he's been there to help us
and I know he will, you see.

I marvel at my husband; what a
good man he turned out to be,
thank You, dear Father
for sending him to me.

This was written on our forty-fifth Anniversary to May 24, 2002. I could dedicate this story to everyone I came in contact with during my years of service. First on my egg route. Then my Meals on Wheels route, and finally on my service to Burnett County EOF. But I would like to mention three special people, ladies that come to mind. Mable Christenson provided a very fond memory for me. When I would lightly sit her lap and she would bounce me, nobody ever did that to me in my life. Thanks, Mabel. I hope it brought back a memory for her too. I appreciated a lady named Hannah Lein. She took such good care of my great-aunt Sara Harvey. She was losing her eyesight, so Hannah was a great help to her. Aunt Sarah died before I started working at ECF. Thank you, Hannah. You were one of God's angels on earth. The third lad was Margie Hegge; she was an inspiration to me. Sometimes I would feel sorry for myself, but then I'd think of Margie and I'd kick myself in the pants and tell myself, *Maybe you lacked parents to love you, but you had the ability to walk and have a contented life, especially if you wanted it.*

Speaking of love, the one person who loved me was my father, and because of Grandma, I rejected that love. I learned a painful lesson. Even though I don't have the ability to love, I do have the ability to care deeply about other people. I was never with Dad long enough to form a loving feeling for him. I saw him maybe twice a year while I was growing up, the same with my oldest brother. I didn't see him for thirteen years. When Neil went back to Dad, I didn't see him very often either. So the negative lessons I learned as a child, I am not passing them down to my children, grandchildren, or great-grandchildren. I have a great deal of affection for my family, and I hope that makes up for any negative feelings I have for what cousins I have left.

Speaking of cousins, my cousin Helen Rose, when she was a little girl, got hit by a car who passed by a school bus that was stopped and had the stop sign out. One of her legs was shattered. I don't know about the other leg. Her leg was so bad, and she was so little they had to put a plate in her leg because her bones were growing. The citizens of Chippewa County got a petition and took it to Madison. Because of Helen's accident, I hope many school children all over our country don't have to go through what Helen did; that is a very good law.

I hope whoever reads this story will find comfort in it. It's meant to be an inspiration to anyone who had a similar life or to anyone lucky enough to have parents who love them. I forgave my grandma for the things she said and did.

I tried taking care of Angil, but my knees were getting bad and I can't move fast enough to catch her when she got away from me. She figured out how to get out of my apartment and run the elevator to get out of this building. If she got outside in the winter and I couldn't get her back inside, she could freeze to death. It was too dangerous for me to keep her. She was no longer safe here with me.

I'm so grateful for the people who care for my granddaughters, Brian and Theresa Anderson; the family that loves and nurtures Angil, and also to David and Lois Hemingway, the family that does the same thing for Melina.

Although Dianne is a better mother and grandmother than I will ever be, I was not a good example as a mother, and I did not teach my kids what kids should learn. They pretty much raised themselves. I wanted them to be independent so that if something happened to me, they would be all right. My thinking was way off. I should have given them a stable base so when something happened to me or their dad, they would be strong and okay.

My granddaughters are with good stable families. I thank God for good Christian people. I have a strong faith in Christ, but I tend to be lazy in practicing going to church on a regular basis. Any ability to write, either poetry or music, I give all credits to my heavenly Father.

The first book of poetry I wrote, I ended it with the poem "Forgiveness," which was a very fitting poem to end the book with. Forgiveness is a great healer. At least it was, in my case. As long as I carried that albatross on my shoulders, I couldn't do anything. When I made peace with God, Grandma, and anyone else that I needed to forgive, that burden was gone; and I felt my creative juices start flowing. Jesus did that for me. When I get the urge to write, words just flow. That's God's hand on me. I cannot do anything on my own. We all need Christ in our lives every day. Amen.

# Forgiveness

I learned to forgive my grandma
for some things she said to me,
I understand her state of mind
and now my mind is free.

This poem is my safety valve. If things get to me, I remember these few words. I intended to end this book at this point, but I woke up during the night and the word *love* kept going around in my head. That is one feeling that I am not very familiar with. I don't know the meaning of the word. I had very little knowledge of love while I was growing up. I was very insecure when I was a child. I didn't trust anyone, and I was not a loveable child, so I had no one to guide me.

I lost both parents at bad times in my life, one to death and the other because he was not capable of raising us. Also the lies Grandma told me, so I was scared of him. I saw Dad maybe once or twice a year. The time I spent with him was of little value. I think that love is an emotion that starts very early in life, and if it's not nurtured, it doesn't get a chance to grow.

I like people and can show empathy toward them. I suppose that is a form of love. I can tell my kids, grandkids, and great-grandkids that I love them, but do I? I am proud of them, but am I capable of love? I don't know the answer to that one. I can't remember anyone showing me any kind of caring while growing up, except Dad. He used to hug me, and I rejected him because Grandma told me if I got in the car with him, he would kidnap me and take me back to Cornell and the welfare would put me in an orphanage. She scared me with horror stories about what they do to kids there. This is the torment that has followed me a good share of my life. I married my husband right out of high school. It was a way to escape from a bad situation at home, not a good reason to marry, but I felt comfortable and happy when I was with him. I suppose that was a form of love also. We were married forty-seven years when he died. He was the best friend I ever had. He used to drive me crazy; he was as stable as I was unstable, but he and his folks and sister were the best people to deal with me. And believe me, they had their hands full. I wanted to be in the family group, but I also needed to be independent and do things by myself, like berry picking. That was a big problem with them.

I was not a very loving mother to my kids. I taught them to be strong and depend on themselves. They are good people, and I am proud of them. I was not the best grandmother to Donna and Chucky either, but they had a loving mother to guide them. When I got custody of Angil, my first great-granddaughter, I knew I was in trouble. I knew early on I was not good for her. My old insecurities reared their ugly head. I knew she was not safe with me in my second floor apartment. She would get up on the bed and stand on the window sill with only a flimsy screen between her and the ground two floors down. I thought it would only be a matter of time before she would fall through the screen and onto the ground.

Both Angil and Melina are in good hands in loving Christian homes, and I am so grateful for that. I thank God there are people who are willing to take foster kids and treat them like family. God bless them for giving those precious little girls a good start in life. I knew I wasn't capable to do that.

Dianne could do it, but she has health problems, both knees replaced, and she has lung problems. My son Dan is unmarried, and he works at the veteran's hospital. The girls love Uncle Chuck, but he is young and unmarried, and he works the night shift so that wouldn't work out.

The girl's parents have problems and are not capable of rearing young children. Hopefully, the girls will be well grounded and able to fend for themselves by the time they can make their own decisions. I hope my dysfunctional family that started with my parents will finally end with my great-grandkids.

My daughter and her son are fine now. My grandson is coming along fine now. Donna needs help yet. As for me, I am trying to get rid of a lot of baggage. I think I'm doing okay, and then sometimes a memory will come back to torment me. I feel myself slipping backward. This time though, instead of crawling in a bottle of wine, I turn to my Savior and He shelters me so I feel safe again. He makes me capable to put this down on paper. Thank You, Jesus. I know there is no problem that He can't handle. What a comfort.

## Demons

I have two little demons that I battle with every day. If I let my guard down, they could defeat me very easily. Demon Number 1 is alcohol. I fight drinking every day; if I'd take one drink of wine, I'd drink the whole bottle. The other demon is casinos or anywhere there are slot machines. I even try to stay away from the legion hall because of the machines there.

A few years ago on a hot summer day, I thought wine coolers would taste good. I bought a four pack. The first day, I drank one bottle. The next day, I drank the other three, so that gave me my answer. If I go to the casino, I will spend all my cash, then I will tap into my checking account. As a last resort, I'll use my credit card. I get possessed; maybe the next pull will give me a huge jackpot, almost never happens. I fight those two demons every day. I am fine, but it's a struggle. Again, Jesus is my refuge. Amen.

If I ask questions of my grandma about death or other questions like, where do babies come from? She would tell me, "Don't talk about that. It's not nice." So I was afraid of death and almost everything else.

I married a man who was almost as green as I was, so we learned about babies and such together. He was the only partner I had, and it was the same for him as far as I know.

I'm a mixed-up person in a lot of ways. I am just as determined to give my best if I believe in something. For example, I had an egg route that I had for a number of years, Meals on Wheels, for thirty-two years; and I worked at the nursing home for fifteen years until I fell on ice and hurt my shoulder. It still bothers me to this day. In 1997, I started with Meals on Wheels again. It has been thirteen years this stretch. I was a driver for Mrs. Hammergren for eight years from 1968 to 1976. Dianne lived with her from 1976 to 1981. I have no intention of giving up my meal route as long as I am able to do it. So far, my mind is okay, but my knees are not so good. I need the people I see each day. They inspire me, and I get creative ideas from my work. We provide a service. My daughter and I hope we can keep on for a long time. With God's help, we can. My husband was a faithful servant also. In the fifteen years I worked at ECF, he did the route. When I left ECF, we split the route so he did the route about seventeen years. When he got sick, Dianne took his route. She's been involved about thirteen years. I've been involved about seventeen years. When Ruben died on the morning of June 4, 2004, I went on my meal route as usual. People asked me how I could do that. My answer, "Ruben would expect it of me." He was that dedicated, and I respected him enough to do what he would expect and want me to do.

# My Pretty Dress

My mama crocheted a dress
for me many years ago,
a pretty turquoise color
with black ribbon with a bow.

Although it was unfinished
when Jesus called her home,
a friend of hers completed it
and it was my dress alone.

That dress is a treasure
that mama made for me,
I take from its storage
place it beauty to see.

I took my daughter's picture
when she was four years old,
wearing my pretty dress
what a story that picture told.

Also my granddaughter
wore my pretty dress,
three generations my
dress was surely blessed

although it's getting older
and the color not as bright
as when my mama made it for me
oh, what a comforting sight.

I think of Mama often
her face I'd live to see,
I'd tell her that I love her
and cuddle her close to me.

I know someday I'll see her
and maybe we'll sing a song,
and praise our loving Savior
for making us so strong.

What prompted this poem was my idea to bring it to my apartment. I brought my dress and my little basket that my mom gave to me when I was a child. She died sixty-seven years ago so that basket has been in my care for between sixty-seven and seventy-one years. If the basket was new or secondhand, I have no idea or how old it is. It is the only thing I have from my mother, except for my dress. The basket is etched glass.

Here is a sweet little poem.

# A Child's Wish

Daddy, please tell me
where did my mommy go,
I need to see her
I really need to know.

I need her to hold me
and kiss me goodnight,
and tell me she loves me
and make things all right.

These are questions asked
by a little girl,
who lost her mother and
upset her little world.

# The Silence of the Birds

The birds were singing loudly as
they greeted the coming dawn,
but now they are silent I wonder
where they have gone.

I don't see any movement in the
tree outside my place,
earlier they were so busy
so full of life and grace.

Maybe they are resting some
place outside my sight,
I hope they will be returning
sometime before tonight.

It is supposed to be hot and sticky
not my favorite kind of day,
I'm looking for a lovely fall
I hope summer goes away.

I heard a solitary goose
what a mournful sound,
maybe headed for Memory Lake
on the west side of town.

DONNA SHOGREN

It's evening and the birds are
back as noisy as can be,
discussing their busy day
in their lovely leafy tree.

# Paintings

The country is like a painting
with many shades of green,
and each area you travel
you see a different scene.

You go across a meadow
and you see a lovely blue,
that is the water
and the shores a different hue.

The dark green of the stately pines
the oaks a lighter green,
If I were an artist
I'd paint that lovely scene.

I can't paint a picture with a
brush; why? I cannot guess,
but I can paint a picture with words
for it works the best.

# Blessings

Bless the words, dear Father
As I slowly write them down,
and please tell me what to say
when my mind has run aground.

I never thought of our northern
states with the humid jungle heat,
it is so oppressing; it can
knock you on your seat.

In the winter, we have winds chills
heat index is our summer curse,
I don't know which is better
or which is the worse.

I wonder if we're being tested
to see how much we can take,
to see just how strong we are
how much before we break.

I know Jesus loves us and
I know He does His best,
to teach us what we should know
He is so fair and just.

# Canadian Geese

I saw some gees today
sitting on a dock,
not very many
it was a little flock.

They looked so comfortable
standing in the sun,
the geese in the water
only numbered one.

It gave me much pleasure
to see that delightful sight,
it seemed so natural, and
it also seemed just right.

They didn't seem disturbed
as I slowly drove on by,
I hope to see them tomorrow
at least I'm going to try.

# Acorns

The acorns are falling from
a mighty oak tree,
all the food on the ground
not one squirrel do I see.

If they had a pantry
soon it would be filled,
against the long winter months
with the snow and the chill.

So I'm going to take some acorns
and do my very best,
to try to grow some oak trees
I hope I pass the test.

# Miracles

I see a new miracle
every day that I live,
I thank You, dear Father
for every lovely gift.

The miracle of the sunshine
and every fluffy cloud
and every single choir and
the song they sing out loud.

Thank You for the lovely moon
and every twinkling star
it must be so beautiful
Father where You are.

Thank You for the miracle
of every single birth,
be it human or animal
that lives upon this earth.

Thank You for putting love
and compassion in our hearts,
but we have a long way to go
but at least it is a start.

Please forgive all the people
who did that awful deed,
speak to their hearts, dear Lord
they have a very great need.

They all need to correct
the errors of their ways,
and ask for peace and forgiveness
for the rest of their days.
Dianne, the Mechanic

I like to watch my daughter
every move so sure and sound
she knows what she is doing
as she sits upon the ground.

She had some good teachers
throughout the many years,
first her father and then her husband
she tackles jobs without fear.

They both are good teachers
in their own special way,
but she has much common sense
many times she's saved my day.

I appreciate my daughter
she certainly is a gem,
I wish everyone was as lucky
we could some more of them.

I'm proud of my daughter
she has a loving heart,
she loves her kids and grandkids
though I gave her a rocky start.

# Memories of Mama

My memories of Mama
are few and far between,
I knew she was human
but to me, she was a queen.

I put her on a pedestal
way above the rest,
I know she had her faults
but to me, she was the best.

In my mind, I hear her laughter
and I see her sparkling eyes,
and I feel her warm loving arms
when I hurt myself and cried.

Although my memories are
precious and mean a lot to me,
It's not like the real thing
not the way it ought to be.

Someday we'll be together
when we do not know,
that is up to Jesus; He
knows when it's time to go.
Memories of a Country Girl

The memories of a country girl
flood my very soul,
they make me feel young again
although my age is old

Some memories are so bitter
some memories are so sweet,
together they balance out
and to me that very neat.

We had a lot of neighbors
some were kin some were friends,
but we are all one family
with God until the end.

Once a year, I go traveling
on the land where I did walk,
just me and my memories
I don't even need to talk.

I remember the berries
and the water in the creek,
the peace and the solitude
I felt so small and meek.

# Angel Eyes

In my mind, I see my angel's
eyes looking at me with love,
she was sent to me to guide my
steps from Jesus up above.

I see my pretty angel with
wings made out of gold,
she shelters me within those
wings she soothes my very soul.

Someday I'll see her in person
though to me, she's very real,
I'll see her pretty smile
and her golden wings I'll feel.

We all need an angel we
can tell our troubles to,
between her and Jesus
together, they'll see us through.

So I'll be patient, sweet angel
until I see your pretty face,
and I'll see your wings and halo
and your amazing grace.
The Spirit of God

The Spirit of God
is guiding my pens,
as I write many words
it seems without end.

He is patiently waiting
in the corner of my mind,
when I get in trouble
He's loving and kind.

He puts in my mind
what He wants me to say,
I thank my dear Father
for that every day.

I know we can trust Him
and we should do our best,
to follow His teachings
until it's time to rest.

When I think of Jesus
and I imagine His face,
I see His beauty
kindness and grace.

He is so special
God's only Son,
I feel so unworthy
and I will to the end.
Praise the Lord! Amen.

# Leaves

The rustle of the fallen leaves
is music to my ears,
sound like angels singing
the sound so soft but clear.

The wind playing in the swaying
boughs is a lovely sight to see,
caressing each other
so soft but tenderly.

They tremble when a gusty
breeze sends them on their way,
some leaves will stay just where
they are; maybe they'll fall another day.

# Turtles

Turtles are amazing creatures
that move slowly on their way,
they take their house wherever
they go they have no rent to pay.

If they are in danger
they go into their home,
and stay there for a little
while cozy, safe, and warm.

## Chip and Sadie

Chip and Sadie were two dogs that lived with a lady named Helen.
She lived off Highway 87, a couple miles or so. I took dinners to her
for quite some time. She lived in a country home and had cornfields
close by.

Chip was a black Lab. I don't know what breed Sadie was, if
she was lab or not; she was an off-white color. When I would deliver
meals to Helen, the cooks would send out dark bread once in a while.
I didn't care for mine, so I gave it to the two dogs. Chip at his bread,
but Sadie would bury hers in the cornfield. It didn't stay their long;
Chip would go out there and dig it up. I wrote a poem about it. I
think a friend has the book that the poem is in. I have fond memories
of Chip and Sadie. They were two of God's four-legged angels.

I don't remember why I wrote this poem. I don't know if I wrote
it for a particular person, people in general, or myself. Some of the
verses fit me very well.

# Troubled

I know a little girl
she has a troubled mind,
she needs your help, dear Jesus
I know You're loving and kind.

We don't know what the problem
is or how she is this way,
I beg you, dear Father, please
help her every day.

She needs your help so badly
help her to understand,
lead her gently, dear Father
please take her by the hand.

She needs a miracle
that only You can do,
I ask for her, dear Father
please guide her whole life through.

She is so pretty what a
creation You did make,
and she can be so gentle
but she makes many mistakes.

DONNA SHOGREN

She has a nasty temper, but
You know her better than I,
I beg you to help her, Lord
and we should also try.

She is one of your children
please show her mercy and love,
her problems will over when
she joins You in heaven above.

# Frogs

I love to hear a bunch of frogs
croaking in a pond,
communicating in a language
only they can understand.

# Nighttime Singers

One night I heard a whippoorwill
singing to his heart's delight,
when he started doing his thing
he gave me quite a fright.

I thought he was inside my house
his voice so loud and clear,
but he was next to our chimney
that my he sounded so near.

I listen to that unique bird sing
the notes are almost the same,
he's one of God's singers; among
the birds, he will surely reign.

I miss the sound of the whippoorwill
I heard it for many years,
but in town, its voice is silent
it almost brings me to tears.

# Twenty-Five Years

Twenty-five years ago
I became your wife,
I thank God everyday
for sending you into my life.

If we have some problems
as we do from time to time,
we solve them together
I am yours and you are mine.

We've walked together down the
path of life each and every day,
may we continue walking together
for the rest of the way.

So thank you, dear husband
for the many years of love,
and the blessings of our Father
He's guiding us from above.

# Christmas

*C* is for the child born on this day
*H* is for the hay in the manger where he lay
*R* is for riches the wise men brought that day
*I* is for inspiration that helps us on our way
*S* is for the Savior our Father up above
*T* is for truth about His lasting love
*M* is for Mary the mother of our Lord
*A* is for always His love we can't afford
*S* is for our Savior who loves us as we
are even though we are sinners and
He's watching from afar.

This is the way that Jesus told my mind that this is a good description of what Christmas is all about. Thank You, dear Lord, our heavenly Father.

# October Day

The sun is kind of hazy on
this lovely October day,
I suppose it won't be long
before winters here to stay.

The geese and cranes are gathering
for the trip they'll have to take,
to a much warmer climate
it's one they yearly make.

They wait for the signal that
Mother Nature sends,
and then begins their journey
many miles before it ends.

So guide their flight, dear Father
and keep them in Your sight,
until we see them once again
on their yearly northern flight.

There are huge flocks of cranes
picking up kernels of grain,
preparing for their yearly trek
each year it's still the same.

# Method to My Madness

There's a method to my madness
in regards to my car,
I deliberately keep it cluttered
I think I should be a star.

If I get rid of all the stuff
I'd soon get some more,
I can still me my ceiling
but I can't find my floor.

Maybe someday I'll clean it
when the danger is through,
I think that's a find idea
I think that's what I'll do.

But where to store my treasure
it boggles my puny mind,
I'm running out of storage space
nooks and crannies are hard to find.

# Guard Dog

Hello, my name is Princess
my size is kind of small,
but the love I have in my
heart makes be big and tall.

I have one important job
it means a lot to me,
and that is guarding Angil
she's a baby, don't you see?

The moment that I see her
then my job begins,
and that is guarding Angil
she has such silky skin.

Sometimes I get sleepy
while doing my important job,
I sneak a little cat nap
when my head begins to nod.

Angil is now four years old
Princess is in doggy heaven.

# Dancing Leaves

I was lying in bed relaxing
and thinking about my days,
I was looking out my window
as the wind began to play.

The leaves and branches of a mighty
tree began swaying far and near,
they dance in perfect rhythm
to music only they can hear.

And then it gets so quiet
no movement anywhere,
and then they start dancing again
the music they gladly share.

I saw a bird go flying by
I wonder what he thinks,
about his dancing weaving home
when the wind plays its tricks.

# Flying

I wish I could fly like and eagle
riding along on a breeze,
I'd go where ever I wanted
I'd land where ever I'd please.

I'd see a lot of country; some
place I'd never seen before,
I'd glide for many miles
and then I'd fly some more.

I'd fly until I was tired, and
then I'd glide some more,
I don't need any directions; I'd
follow the path of my Lord.

I'd land in the tallest tree
and survey the turf below,   ·
I'd see what ever there was to see
and then it is time to go.

# Nature

Nature is a treasure to be
enjoyed by one and all,
from the tiniest little flower
to the trees so big and tall.

To the littlest stream of water
to the rivers deep and wide,
the sight of both of them can
fill me with awe and pride.

To the tiny little kittens
so helpless and alone,
makes one so protective
but nature provides a home.

to watch a brand new mother
as she cuddles her babies near,
I wander at the instincts God
gave her the trust and the fear.

To see a baby fawn as it
tries to stand alone,
it's legs start to tremble
but soon it feels at home.

# MY LIFE IN A NUTSHELL

To see a flock of baby geese
the number large or small,
are important to their parents
they are their babies one and all.

I watched the faithful mother swan
atop her nest so high,
the partners of the lovely bird
is something we can't deny.

Sometimes back in my memory
I'm a child once again,
walking in the forest
the creek my only friend.

Those times were so special
it was my time to dream,
About what I wanted to do
where I fit in nature's scheme.

Even now I'm still learning
to trust my Lord above,
to treasure different people
and show them faith and love.

No matter how old we get
and life passes us by,
we have a lot of living to
do before it's time to die.

# Thank You, Lord

Thank You for the clouds on high
thank You for the clear blue sky
thank You for the birds that sing
thank You, Lord, for everything.

Thank You for the food we eat
thank You for the honey so sweet
thank You for the friends we meet
thank You, Lord, for every treat.

Thank You for my grandkids, Lord
thank You for my little Ford
thank You for the deep blue sea
thank You for the lovely trees.

Thank You for the flowers so sweet
thank You for everyone we meet
thank You for the rains that fall
thank You for the trees so tall.

Thank You for the berries so sweet
thank You for the fruit we eat
thank You for the songs we sing
thank You, Lord, for everything.

# Squirrels

I was talking to a squirrel
on a sunny blustery day,
I did a lot of talking
but he didn't have much to say.

He was looking for some dinner
as he traveled to and fro,
I watched him till he was out of
sight; Mr. Squirrel, where did you go?

Maybe I'll keep on searching
until I see him again,
I hope he'll find some acorns
before the day comes to an end.

# Heaven

I'd like to take a little stroll
down streets paved in gold,
I'd walk with my Savior
and His disciples of old.

He'd teach us some lessons
on how things ought to be,
how we should love our
neighbors, friends, and family.

Someday we'll all be standing
outside those pearly gates,
when Jesus says, "Please enter"
won't that day be great?

We'll see our friends and loved
ones who died so long ago,
one big happy family
together forever more.

Following is a series of little poems I wrote. Some are some are a little longer. I call them "Family Gems."

# Family Gems

My dad was a treasure I
never knew I had,
until it was way too late
and that is very sad.

My mother died at thirty-four
left three small children alone,
Dad tried his best to raise his kids
to provide us with a home.

I looked up to my big brother
he stood six feet three,
we weren't raised together
but he meant the world to me.

To Neil, I was a nuisance
who bugged him now and then,
If we'd been raised as sibling
he could have been my friend.

Uncle Ralph was our singer
and guitar player too,
he taught me how to yodel
and rearrange a song or two.

Aunt Edith was Mom's sister
the only one she had,
she tried to do the best she could
but she always seems so sad.

This verse is not exactly or actually the truth. In the last several years of his life, he had several strokes, and everyone he had made him more sarcastic; and he'd say hurtful things. Toward the end, I didn't ever want to see him. He's the same uncle that said hurtful things to me when he'd been drinking. He died in 1965.

Uncle Judd was full of mischief
you never knew what he'd do,
I loved him like a father
until his life was through.

I know my grandma tried to
the very best she could,
but why she was so nasty
I never understood.

She was mean to Aunt Edith
she said some hurtful things,
she worshipped my mother
she was perfect like a ring.

I grew up not knowing
where on earth I should be,
but forty-one years
ago, we found a place for me.

I am a country bumpkin
and I have been all my life,
and I'm perfectly content to
be a country bumpkin's wife.

One of my favorite wild flowers is the wild rose; the scent of that flower is so pure and sweet. We have wild roses growing on different roads, sometimes right through the blacktop.

I like the lupines, sweet williams, lilac, and especially the beautiful trilliums.

# Bald Eagle

I saw a bald eagle sitting
on a branch of a tree,
surveying his surroundings
to see what he can see.

As I approached his resting place
he suddenly took flight,
I wonder about the creature
that came into his sight.

He took off just like an arrow
a wondrous sight to see,
I'm glad I wasn't his target
I wouldn't want him to eat me.

I marvel at his eyesight
how keen it must be,
how God must love the eagle
to set the eagle free.

# Rectangle

I think of my body as a rectangle
from my shoulder to my seat,
my heads at the top of the rectangle
the bottom is my legs and feet.

My arms are another addition
one on each side of my shape,
I'm one big rectangle
what a familiar trait.

I have problems with all
four corners of my rectangle,
my shoulders and my knees
I'm ok in the middle I'm easy to please.

I have some extra bulges
I have had all my life,
but I'm fat and happy
I spent forty-seven years as a wife.

I wish my rectangle was smaller
and a little lighter too,
but I'm also getting older
my life is almost through.

I also have two working hands
they have done a lot through the years,
rocked several babies
and wiped many tears.

They have milked many cows
two quarters at a time,
I'm glad a cow only has one tail
that suits me just fine.

I have a nice little family
they are a treasure to me,
we're four generations
a sturdy family tree.

## Turkeys

Turkeys, the wild ones, are another wonder I see on my meal route.
One day two of us had to stop our cars on Highway 87. I was going
north, the other driver south. A flock of twenty-four turkeys walked
single file between us. They trusted us, but we were tempted to drive
on. Wild turkeys can fly away, but domestic turkeys can't fly.

# Mirages

On a hot summer day
is when mirages appear,
the appearance of water
shows up shiny and clear.

The closer you get, then
it fades from your sight,
and it shows up again
shiny and bright.

The sun on the black top
is the cause of this thing,
a mirage is so strange
much wonder it brings.

When the days get cooler
then the mirage will go,
and come back next summer
that fact we all know.

## Miracles

I believe in miracles. When God is in charge, it happens every time
a baby is born, be it human or nonhuman. How a little acorn can
become a giant oak is a miracle and how a pine cone can become a
stately pine tree.

How a small little four-year-old orphan who was lost without parents—one by death and the other, not capable of raising her—turned into a bitter bully in the grade school years who was a lost, wandering being and who married a caring man that didn't know what he was getting into and who saw in me something worth keeping. We had two kids that grew up to be two beautiful caring adults in spite of my neglect and my inability to be a good parent. Thank God their father and his parents were stable.

My faith in God got me through the years of my turmoil. I rebelled at many things. When I finally hit rock bottom, I gave in and surrendered to God. I gave up my destructive habits, wine, and casinos, being the worst. After that, I gave up my hatred and bitterness toward Grandma. I was then able to write poetry, lyrics, and music and even this autobiography. This is the greatest miracle God put in place. I am proud of the things that I was able to accomplish with God's guidance.

This journey has been good for me. I held my feelings in check for so long it was destroying me. Grandma sure did a good job on me. I hope whoever reads this will find some comfort in it. I can't change the past and my lack of relationship with my parents and brothers, but I can and do change my relationship with my daughter, son, my grandkids, and my great-granddaughters.

I keep in touch with my cousin Roger; I don't know how many of the others are still living, and I talk to my sister-in-law and her family from time to time.

The one Rock I give credit to for changing me is my heavenly Father. He had a great deal to do with my writing this book. When I was stuck, He took over and gave me the words. Thank You, Jesus.

We had quite a snow storm last weekend, and I was sitting in the car while my daughter went into the store for a few things. Here is a poem I wrote about that day.

# The Miracle of the Snowflake

The miracle of the snowflake
is hard to comprehend,
that six-sided wonder
will miracles never end.

I'm watching the snowflakes
as they fall gently from the sky,
each one is different
I'm not going to question why

My mind cannot understand
the number that will fall
in all of the world
when winter comes to call.

The designer of the snowflake
and all the people who have lived,
performed the greatest miracles
what love our Father gives. Amen.

This book shows how much I love our Lord. He guides me every day.
He knows me better than I know myself, and He loves me in spite of
my many faults. Thank You, Jesus.

Love,
Your Servant,
Donna Shogren

# Heaven's Door

An angel opened up the door
But she didn't invite me in,
I said, I came to see Jesus
He is my greatest Friend.
They carefully checked the records
Looking for my name,
They found I never rejected Him
So they won't do the same.

So please don't reject Him
We need Him every day,
He is the way to heaven
There is no other way.

—Donna Shogren

This is a new poem I have written a short time ago.

# Robins

Where do the Robins go
When winter comes to call?
I hope in a milder place
When the wind starts to howl.

I can imagine the journey
The miles they must fly,
To get to warmer weather
To stay here they'd probably die.

I know in the springtime
When the Robins appear,
To see the Robin's red breasts
It fills my heart with cheer.

The strength of that little bird
When the time comes to fly,
It's all up to its Maker
I will never question why.

# About the Author

Donna Shogren is an eighty-one-year-old woman who loves God and thanks Him for giving her the ability to write.